‹
Ti.
r
c
nds
nce
ORG.
ses t
lder
writi
me
a b
Man
pro
bu
er

h,
t o.

his
ed
ter
ing
t, V
arag   l
slatio   b
rful l   age h
cura   as

short
der, t
ged v
hurch

WERCKMEISTER'S ORGELPROBE
IN ENGLISH

WERCKMEISTER'S

ERWEITERTE
UND
VERBESSERTE
ORGELPROBE
IN ENGLISH

TRANSLATED BY

GERHARD KRAPF

RALEIGH: AT THE SUNBURY

1976

Library of Congress Cataloging in Publication Data

Werckmeister, Andreas, 1645-1706.
  Werckmeister's Erweiterte und verbesserte Orgel-Probe in English.
    1. Organ—Construction.   I. Title.
ML552.W413   786.6'3   76-21064
ISBN 0-915548-03-8

Printed for The Sunbury by Bynum Printing Company, Raleigh.

Andreæ Werckmeisters
Benic. Cheruscip. t. Musici
und Organisten an S. Martini
in Halberstadt.

Erweiterte und vermehrte
Orgel-Probe.

Quedlinburg.
In Verlegung Theodori
Phil. Calvisii.
Aō 1698.

ANDREÆ Werckmeisters/

Benic. Cherusci, p. t. Musici und Organ. zu S. Martini
in Halberstadt

Erweiterte und verbesserte

Orgel=Probe/

Oder

Eigentliche Beschreibung/

Wie und welcher Gestalt man die Orgelwercke von
den Orgelmachern annehmen/ probiren/ untersuchen und
denen Kirchen liefern könne; Auch was bey Verdüngniß
eines neuen und alten Wercks/ so da zu renoviren
vorfallen möchte/nothwendig in acht zu
nehmen sey/

Nicht nur einigen Organisten / so zu probirung
eines Orgelwercks erfodert werden/zur Nachricht: Son-
dern auch denen Vorstehern / so etwan Orgeln
machen oder renoviren lassen wollen/
sehr nützlich:

Jetzo von dem AUTORE selbst übersehen/mit gründlichen Uhrsachen
bekräfftiget/ und zum Druck befordert.

Qvedlinburg/

In Verlegung THEODORI PHILIPPI CALVISII,
Buchhändlers daselbst.
Gedruckt bey Joh. Heinrich Sievert/ F.S.Hoff=Buchdr.
Anno 1698.

Andreas Werckmeister's

— Musician and Organist at St. Martin in Halberstadt —

Enlarged and Improved

[handbook on]

ORGAN-PROOFING

OR

DETAILED DESCRIPTION OF

How and by which methods to accept, test and examine organ builders' instruments for delivery to churches; further, what must be considered in contracting for the construction of new organs or the renovation of old instruments; not only for the information of organists retained as consultants, but also for the benefit of officials contemplating the construction of new organs or the renovation of old instruments.

Revised, strengthened by factual arguments

and released for printing by the author.

Quedlinburg

issued by Theodor Philipp Calvisius, book dealer.

printed by Johann Heinrich Sievert, court printer.

1 6 9 8 .

[TABLE OF CONTENTS]

[For the convenience of the reader, Werckmeister's sometimes verbose language in this table of contents occasionally has been abridged. No page numbers are given in the original.]

Chapter 1
First of all, contract must be studied. Who should proof organs. Inspecting bellows and bellows housing........................ 1

Chapter 2
Inspecting the pipe work for proper quality. Chimney flutes 3

Chapter 3
Further description of pipe work. How to maintain pipes to ensure longevity. Inspecting mixtures................................... 4

Chapter 4
Description of reeds; resonators; shallots; reeds; tuning wires; blocks 5

Chapter 5
Inspecting wind chests, particularly top boards, bearers, sliders, pallets, and so forth.. 7

Chapter 6
Further discussion of wind chest inspection. Trade secrets of organ builders.. 10

Chapter 7
Action; stop action rollers; roller boards; roller boards pins; keyboards and the like.. 11

Chapter 8
Quality of wind chest construction; terminology, *e.g.* frame, bars, key channels; drilled chest; pallets; table; bearers; topboards; pipe rack. Brief description of spring chest.. 12

Chapter 9
The question of measuring the pipes. The layout of keyboards and pedal board... 15

CONTENTS

CHAPTER 10
Aural examination, *e.g.* depressing all keys simultaneously. Acceptable limit of runs. Testing accuracy of slider holes 17

CHAPTER 11
Individual examination of stops 18

CHAPTER 12
Ensemble testing of two and more stops. Sufficiency of wind. Why some organ builders prefer low wind pressure. Wind shaking, its main cause; big wind consumption by pipes 20

CHAPTER 13
Individual stop examination by major thirds; detecting runs. The *wolf*. Causes of impure tuning. Why organs are rarely in tune 25

CHAPTER 14
Subbass and Unterstaz; their construction. Why pipes of narrow and wide scale sounding together go quickly out of tune. Basic concepts of scaling. Wide scales produce pompous, full sound; narrow scales produce gentle sound 28

CHAPTER 15
Reed stops; their resonance. Good reeds stay in tune with tremulant 29

CHAPTER 16
Tremulant; couplers; Zimbelstern 30

CHAPTER 17
Miscellaneous testing procedures; evaluation of the spring chest 31

CHAPTER 18
Further discussion of the spring chest; construction 32

CONTENTS

CHAPTER 19
Manual and pedal transmission. Faulty bellows construction; uneven wind, a nuisance............................34

CHAPTER 20
Testing for even wind without a wind gauge? What to look for in the bellows................................36

CHAPTER 21
Contracting for an organ. Organ specification. Evaluation of the *Tierce, i.e.* thus falsely called Sesquialtera. Caution regarding specifying too many reeds. Faulty and incomplete specifications. Annotated specification of a large organ; how to derive a smaller specification from it. Whole, half and quarter organs. Stop nomenclature................................38

CHAPTER 22
Low F sharp and G sharp must be built. Short octaves, a source of trouble, and an unfortunate convention................47

CHAPTER 23
Need for detailed specifications in contract. Organ placement, not too close to wall. Supervision of construction............48

CHAPTER 24
Contracting for renovation. Caution regarding replacement of good by inferior matter. Identification in contract of all defects................................49

CHAPTER 25
Organ builders should not overcharge; churches should not be miserly. The construction of the wind gauge..................51

CHAPTER 26
Itemizing pipe weight. Metal alloys. Common good goes before private profit. Collusion between organ proofer and builder. Examination fees................................54

xi

CONTENTS

CHAPTER 27
Coverup of incompetent construction by church officials. Obligations of examiner and church officials in handling observed defects..57

CHAPTER 28
Handling of minor defects; fairness to builder...................................58

CHAPTER 29
On registration. *Aequalstimmen*. Registration and the experienced organist..59

CHAPTER 30
On the correct use of the terms Tierce and Sesquialtera..................61

CHAPTER 31
Maintenance contract; day-to-day maintenance by organist.............63

CHAPTER 32
Qualifications of an organist; hiring procedures. Daily care of organ. A brief discussion of temperament......................64

TRANSLATOR'S PREFACE

Andreas Werckmeister (1645-1706) worked his way from humble beginnings to being recognized as one of Germany's leading music theorists by the turn of the century. The present treatise, *Erweiterte und verbesserte Orgelprobe* (1698) had been preceded by a number of writings which established his reputation, including his first *Orgelprobe* (1681); two printings of *Musicalische Temperatur* (1686-87, 1691); three editions of *Musicae mathematicae Hodegus curiosus* (1686, 1687, 1689); and *Der Edlen Music-Kunst Würde, Gebrauch und Missbrauch* (1691). His thoroughbass treatise was published in the same year as the enlarged *Orgelprobe*, 1698. Although relatively little remains of his compositions, his impressive professional career alone suggests that he must indeed have been a "widely renowned musician and organist," as he was described in the funeral sermon by Pastor Goetze.

Should any doubt remain concerning Werckmeister's practical musicianship, it surely must be dispelled by the contents of this book. Here, he shows himself as the organist-practitioner, for whom whatever sounds and works best takes precedence over any other considerations. Significantly enough, he sees no need to apologize for depending on the practical musician's ear and subjective artistic judgment as the sole criterion. He will even go to such lengths as to admit that "artistic truth" can be "paradox" or — in spite of his considerable scientific and mathematical knowledge — to speak of a "spacious dot," just to explain a practical aspect of tuning. Every sentence breathes intensity, fervor and love for his instrument. He cannot write "without agitation" on aspects of malpractice, and this very personal involvement infuses the book with a breathless spontaneity, whose genuine persuasiveness compensates for occasional redundancies, distracting lack of organization and a few errors of omission. This intensity also ameliorates his moralizing when "gently admonishing the gentlemen of the building trade." The endorsement by one of Germany's foremost organ builders, Arp Schnitger (turned rhymester),* cannot have been lost on his readers.

---

*The late W. L. Sumner's translation of Werckmeister's *Orgelprobe* (Vol. VI, 1-3, 1958) in the now defunct ORGAN INSTITUTE QUARTERLY includes a prose rendition of this poem but omits all other introductory material here included for the benefit of the reader wishing to gain as complete

TRANSLATOR'S PREFACE

In order to present as authentic as possible a text, I have scrupulously refrained from translating interpretively. Where necessary, I have added clarifications in brackets, but all parentheses are Werckmeister's. My footnotes attempt to illuminate the context further. Some periodic constructions in the original German had to be broken down into smaller, more readable English sentences. Punctuation was modernized. The Table of Contents has been condensed and moved to the front of the book, and Werckmeister's list of *errata* was omitted after the corrections had been made in his text. But his organization by paragraphs, all Latin phrases, and his colorful language have been retained as accurately as possible.

I owe a great debt of gratitude to Fritz Noack for reading the typescript as well as the galley proofs, saving me from many inaccuracies, sharing freely with me his store of knowledge and expertise and sparing no time and effort to improve the final version. I am further indebted to the Graduate College of the University of Iowa for financial assistance; and to Mrs. Janet Barrett for her long suffering and excellent work in preparing the typescript from nearly illegible longhand.

G. K.
Iowa City, August 3, 1975

---

as possible an insight even into peripheral aspects of the work. I have attempted to retain the flavor of the time by rendering in rhyme the various dedications. The original German versions read perhaps even more like doggerels.

[PREFACE]

To the most serene Prince and Lord Christian Ludwig, Margrave of Brandenburg, in Prussia, Magdeburg, Cleve, Jülich, Berge, Stettin, Pomerania, of Kashubians and Wends, also in Silesia, Duke of Crossen, Burgrave of Nuremberg, Prince of Halberstadt, Minden and Camin, Duke of Hohenzollern, Marck and Ravensberg, Lord of Ravenstein and of the lands of Lauenburg and Büttau etc.; to the Grandmasters of the Order of the Hospital of St. John; and the Procurators and Archdeacons of Halberstadt, my most gracious Princes and Lords; as well as to the wellborn, most noble, highly esteemed, truly and most learned gentlemen, the President, the Vice Chancellor and the Councillor, appointed to the government and the consistory of the principality of Halberstadt, my sovereign Lords and Patrons.

Most serene and gracious Prince and Lord; wellborn, most noble, highly esteemed, truly and most learned, sovereign Lords and Patrons: Your Serene Princely Highness, most esteemed Magnificence and most learned Grace is surely not unaware of current activities in organ building regarding installations not only in urban but also in humble village churches: It has become increasingly apparent from complaints lodged by many localities that churches and communities are at times ill served by the building trade and are even deceived (as there are few people who understand organ building). Therefore, this little treatise shows not only how an organist might test an organ, but it also offers essential information concerning specifications and materials for every stop along with suggestions to officials dealing with organ installations and repairs. I could not refrain from serving these unfortunate churches and communities with the expertise which God has granted me; the more so, as to my knowledge there is to date no such literature available in print intended for the public benefit. In being so bold as to inscribe and dedicate this little book to Your Serene Princely Highness, most esteemed Magnificence and most learned Grace, I have had no intention presumptuously to aggrandize myself. Rather, because the truth usually arouses hatred, jealousy and persecution, and because my present work might well be a thorn in the sides of a number of incompetent organ builders and bad people, I have desired most submissively and obediently to solicit as patron and protector (next to God) Your Serene Princely

PREFACE

Highness, most esteemed Magnificence and most learned Grace. I most humbly beseech you graciously and favorably to accept and take under your protection this little treatise and to be and remain my gracious and favorable patrons. I am and shall remain

Your Serene Princely Highness'
as well as

Halberstadt,
April 15, 1698

my sovereign Lords' and Patrons'
most submissive and obedient
Andreas Werckmeister
Musician and Organist at
St. Martin in Halberstadt

DEDICATION OF THE FIRST EDITION

Every Christian will perceive in Holy Scripture as well as with faithful and godly people that not only vocal but also instrumental music is well pleasing to God, the Lord, as a means of praise and adoration. In the twenty-fifth chapter of Leviticus, verse 9, and likewise in Numbers 10:2, 10 we find that God himself has ordered the blowing of trombones and trumpets. It is also well known what King David and Solomon thought of and expended on music to the honor of God. In St. John's Revelation 5:8-9 it is reported that the twenty-four elders, each holding a harp, fell down before the Lamb and sang a new song. There we have clear examples for the feasibility of praising and honoring God with instrumental as well as vocal music. It is impossible to name here numerous other examples from Holy Scripture.

I am not unfamiliar with the interpretation of some exegetes who — dismissing the literal meaning of such references — perceive of each Christian as God's spiritual psaltery. In spite of this attractive allegory, however, most teachers of our church do not wish to see the literal meaning perverted. Even though the saintly David has been God's spiritual psaltery, he still used and prescribed for use in the worship service real, physical instruments. Why then should they now be altogether eliminated? I am quite convinced that instrumental music would long have been banned from the church, if it displeased God.[1]

That the patriarchs Basil, Hilary, Justin the martyr, and others highly praised instrumental music in the worship service is amply noted and documented in the excellent Michael Praetorius' [*Syntagma Musicum*, Wolfenbüttel, 1619], Vol. I, p. 135f. Luther, of blessed memory, always very highly esteemed music, as is quite evident from his table talks, the prefaces to several hymnals and his letters, where among other remarks he said: "Music is one of God's beautiful and delightful gifts. Satan is its great enemy, he cannot tolerate it. I have always loved music. He who masters this art is of

---

[1]While organ accompaniment of congregational singing (and presumably also instrumental music) is recorded as early as 1647 in Quedlinburg, Werckmeister here attacks certain contemporary Lutheran tendencies espousing restrictive Reformed attitudes to the use of organ and instruments in the service.

good kind and equipped for everything. Likewise, him who despises music as do all eccentrics, I cannot condone. I give music the highest position and honor next to theology."

This has even been recognized by sagacious heathens who have called music a divine creation, as is reported of Pythagoras, Plato, Socrates and others. They also opined that music, that is to say harmony, originates with the movement of the heavenly bodies which by their respective distance, proportion and motion create harmony. Macrobius[2] cites the example of an elastic rod which, when caused to vibrate slowly, produced a more grave or lower pitch, and a more acute or higher pitch with faster vibrations; he ascribes the same behavior to the progression of heavenly bodies.

This opinion has been shared by many other philosophers and musicians, as one may read with delight in Macrobius' [*Commentarii in somnium Scipionis*] Book 2, chapter 4; Reinhard's and Magister Bartolus'[3] *Musica Mathematica*; likewise Majoragus' *Oratio Musica* and in many other works treating this subject quite beautifully. Dorilaus[4] has written among other statements: *Mundus nihil aliud est, quam Musicum Divinitatis Instrumentum, quia illi concordes in coeli globi dulcissimos emittunt sonos* [the world is nothing else but God's musical instrument, since those concordant bodies of heaven give off the sweetest sounds.]

As to our ear's incapacity to perceive such harmonies, the authors have advanced numerous theories and arguments which for the sake of brevity cannot here be cited.

They agree that man — being *Microcosmus, i.e.* the small world — would be enchanted and delighted by these proportions, if they

---

[2]Ambrosius Theodosius Macrobius (ca. A.D. 44), Latin philosopher and grammarian.

[3]Abraham Bartolus (active in Leipzig ca. 1614). — Werckmeister probably refers to Andreas Reinhard's (active as organist in Schneeberg, 1604) *Musica, sive Guidonis Aretini . . .*, Leipzig, 1604. — Majoragius (according to J. G. Walther's *Musicalisches Lexicon*, 1732) died in 1555.

[4]*Dorilaus* (*i.e.* of Phrygian extraction) might allude to Macrobius' non-Italian origin. As seems to be the case with his preceding Luther quotation, Werckmeister may have paraphrased or quoted from one of countless secondary Neo-Platonist sources, possibly referring to Book I, chapter 14 of Macrobius' *Commentary.*

could be made audible to him by reduction to pure sound; that he
would perceive, as in a mirror, his own image, God's order and the
creatures of heaven and earth, even God's own image in the sense of
the saying, *Omne simile suo simili oblectatur* [every likeness enjoys
its own similarity.]

This nearly tallies with the saying of Holy Scripture in Wisdom
of Solomon 11:22 [*sic*; actually 11:21]: God has ordered all things
with measure, number and weight. Also in chapter 19, verse 17: the
elements interacted as strings of a psaltery sound diversely yet con-
cordantly, this is clearly apparent from this act. Likewise in Job 38:
Do you know who has laid the measures of the earth, when the
morning stars praised me and all the children of God shouted for
joy? Likewise: *Quis enarrabit coelorum rationem & concentum coeli,
quis dormire faciet?*, chapter 35. [Who shall fully describe the system
of the heavens and the heavenly harmony, who shall create as though
sleeping?] More such examples could be cited if time would permit.

For now I shall leave this subject for others to philosophize, and
let those who have occupied themselves with music theory speak to
the question, if music might carry with it divine and supranatural
qualities? On examining the numbers that yield the interval ratios
we find not more than one single additional number, no matter how
many thousand possible calculations one might try, can yield a pure
interval, unless it is related and reduceable to the aforementioned
numbers which contain all consonances and yield the following ratios:

$$\frac{1\quad 2\quad 3\quad 4\quad 5\quad 5\quad 8}{2\quad 3\quad 4\quad 5\quad 6\quad 3\quad 5}$$

How admirably and nicely these ratios operate within the arith-
metic-musical discipline and how on this basis a composition can be
endowed with beautiful and logical order, has been asserted by the
excellent Sethus Calvisius, Lippius, Baryphonus[5] and others. For
this mathematical foundation explains why one tone sounds good
with another, creating a consonance, and why yet another combination does not sound good, producing a dissonance; why one disson-

---

[5]Seth Calvisius (1556-1615), Johannes Lippius (1585-1612), Henricus
Baryphonus (1581-1655), like Werckmeister second-generation Zarlino dis-
ciples, were intrigued by and explored musical *Affekt*.

PREFACE

ance can be resolved and another cannot; why this progression is good, but that must be ruled out; and whatever similar configurations occur in composition that cannot on their outward appearance or by mere aural judgment be fully grasped; the ear assumes the role of yes-man, approving and enjoying what has already been concluded and erected on a solid basis.

The subtle alterations, puzzling yet gratifying one's feeling, that result from contrary motion in musical practice [*"Musica practica,"* as opposed to *musica speculativa*] are familiar to those who have used and thought about this technique. The aforementioned Lippius, a distinguished theologian and excellent musician-mathematician, cannot cease marvelling about musical harmony, God's noble creation. He develops very fine Christian thoughts, *e.g.* comparing the triad with Divine Trinity. Elaborating in detail this and other statements in his third *Musical Discourse* [*Disputatio musica tertia*, Wittenberg, 1610], he exclaims: *En umbram magni illius Mysterii Divinae &* *solum adorandae Trinitatis; Attendat huic Meditationi, quicunque* [*sic*] *Cantilenam Harmonicam vel ipse fingit vel fictam saltem audit; majoris certe aestimabit Musicam* [behold the shadow of that great mystery, Divine Trinity, which alone is to be worshipped: Whoever himself creates, or at least hears harmonious song, should be diligent about it; he surely will appreciate music the more.]; what more could I say (to speak with Luther) the entire matter and value of music are so much greater and richer than one could describe in one brief statement.

Even though music, that noble gift of God, has come to be despised for its misuse, usually associated with gluttonous revelry and, as a result (in the words of another distinguished theologian), has lost that God-given strength and effect which it had possessed in the time of David and other saints, such abuse cannot forever obscure good usage. Therefore, one should not take offense. Touching on this subject, Luther finds that Satan drives such abusers, delinquent youngsters and perverts to their unnatural behavior in order to discredit the noble music (as well as the Word of God) so that the Lord God be deprived of the honor and praise accorded Him by the sound of music. On the other hand, Satan continues to use instruments of his own (people of ill will) in order to frustrate the work of the Lord, for instance when the construction of an organ to the honor of the Lord of hosts is under consideration. When these cannot prevail they slander shamelessly, as most organ builders can testify on the basis of ample experience.

It is true that Satan has advanced to the point where not only church music but also its practitioners and perpetuators find themselves in a deplorable state of contempt since, by and large, they are reduced to a wretched and miserable standard of living by rendering their services. For, alas, nowadays we have come so far that wealth, though at times gained by unjust means, is to be preferred to good arts and virtues.

If Saint David and Solomon were still alive, they would have their Levites better remunerated so as to spare them great cares, anxiety and moaning in the tenure of their office (which is the common complaint at the present time). Whether God could justly continue granting His blessings to congregations which in such manner disparage employment in God's service, is a matter of consideration for judicious people. In most instances the familiar proverb holds true: *Quod non capit Christus rapit Fiscus* [what Christ does not receive, the money bag shall thieve]. But even if a judgment were to be visited upon people, they would remain quite unimpressed and think of it as mere coincidence. It seems to me that the Book of Nehemiah, 13:10, makes a relevant point.[6] It is common knowledge that whenever music is flourishing, the community also maintains prosperity. Did not government along with music enjoy unheard-of success in Solomon's time? Was not the government of Greece in good condition when music was propagated? But after Muhammad had pitched his tent there, music, religion and government together had to exit. Thus became reality Plato's well known dictum: *mutata musica mutatur & Res puplica* [*sic*; when music changes, the State also changes]. Indeed, the oftmentioned M. Praetorius even reports [*op. cit.*] in Vol. II, p. 82, that where music is being spurned and deserted, there religion, as a rule, will also decline.

---

[6] I also found out that the portions of the Levites had not been given to them; so that the Levites and the singers, who did the work, had fled each to his field (Nehemiah 13:10).

PREFACE

Many more such examples could be cited. They all concur that music will gravitate toward God's Word and holy works, and that one must not — as Luther has put it — by Satan's instigation abuse and degrade it.

To summarize: What God has ordained to his service must be held dear and exalted, and through it God's honor must be sought and furthered to the best of mortal man's ability.

Inasmuch as this present little treatise aims precisely at augmenting the praise of God and at contributing to the benefit of church and public, I have no scruples in enlarging and releasing for print this little book; may God graciously grant that it be well used to this end.

AMEN.

PREFACE TO THE KIND READER

As I am aware of having made many enemies with the first edition of my *Organ Proofing* [Frankfurt and Leipzig, 1681], I can easily conclude that by the present edition, in which I am speaking even more pointedly, a greater number of people might be offended, and I foresee an even fiercer onslaught of invective and calumny. But I must herewith assert that I am not at all referring to honest and conscientious organ builders in this little treatise. At any rate, one may expect the best of most builders, just as I have found the majority of organ builders with whom I am acquainted to be honest and trustworthy. But he who feels addressed should reform. He should realize that he acts contrary to God's commandment; that no blessings can be bestowed on dishonest work; indeed, that his descendants will have to disgorge in disgrace and shame all dishonestly earned goods and eventually shall go begging and perish. I do not wish to identify all the unsavory business practices which up to now I have here and there observed, lest anyone be tempted or caused to indulge in these and similar shady tricks. But, once again, I state that I have released this book not as an indictment of, or detriment to, honest and dependable organ builders, but to the glory of God and for use by churches. Meanwhile, I do not begrudge any true artist and artisan his justly earned wages. Moreover, it should be remembered, and I wish so to go on record, that not only the labor but also the artistry rendered by true organ builders ought to be commensurately remunerated. But one must alertly beware of bunglers and botchers, for an organ construction is no small matter; it requires effort and diligence. Now then, since a good intention will inevitably be suspected of ulterior motives, I am quite certain that my well-meaning position will be slandered by many people. But I take little or no stock of this. Those who wish to find fault and jeer will do so anyway, but I have a clear conscience. Indeed, I could not have remained silent about the unethical practices which I have discovered in some organ builders without violating my good conscience, no matter how much it infuriates my detractors. Neither is what I have written fictitious, as some have charged. Rather, it is based on research conducted in the course of well over thirty organ proofings for which I had been engaged. Furthermore, I had some ten organs constructed in my own house at my own expense. Thus, I have good cause for warning my

PREFACE

fellow Christians of occasional malpractice. An intelligent reader will realize that most of my arguments are bolstered by factual evidence, indisputable unless one were to discard natural and conscientious criteria. It should also be noted that this book is neither a treatise nor textbook on organ building. I wish to see everyone use his own building methods and techniques. For one will assert, that a given project might have turned out better with one specific technical approach, another is convinced of the opposite. So long as one can ascertain that this or that invention [imaginative approach] to building promises longevity by all appearances, and that it is well tested by experience, there is no need to dictate to this or the other builder. Let every one work as he pleases. This book does not intend to prescribe specific methods of building to any one. However, I did faithfully describe and disclose, for all who wish and need to know, how an organ must be proofed and what needs to be considered in contracting for organs. Aspiring organ builders may find much incidental information, the better to avoid some of the more common defects. I commend my kind readers to the protection of the Most High and shall remain obliged always to be at their service.

Werckmeister's deftly sketching hand shows here the best
And also points out faults of current organ making,
Which are quite common; yet on this, his strong behest
Many a builder shall henceforth great care be taking.

Out of indebted friendship
these scant but well intentioned lines
were set down by
J. Phil. Bendeler, C. Ord.
in Quedlinburg

How oft has soared aloft human imagination
And wrought such art as does command our adulation?
Could those long departed now awaken, resurrected,
What man has wrought, with awe by them would be detected.
Though music has been used with art and skill forever,
Our own high standard ancients had reached never.

PREFACE

A huge and complex organ one single man can tame
And thousands upon thousands in fervent prayer inflame:
But how could it be so, if defects should abound?
What could an organ do? Outlandish it would sound.
Just take pure harmony away from this fine art,
And see, a ghastly howl is all it will impart.
Now, here Werckmeister* can give us much information,
A master and a man of gifts and education
And of experience! He shows how in detail
New organs one must test and try them without fail.
A worthy task, to be by wise men high commended,
One which shall cause his fame to be richly augmented.
For as posterity this treasure will accept,
His name always among the famous shall be kept.
Of course, some blockhead will find fault, it's not surprising.
Cynics so asinine† can not help criticizing.
But know that only fools this treatise can resent,
While you, dear Werckmeister, to heaven shall ascend.

This has been contributed in

praise of Werckmeister by

Arp Schnitger, Organ Builder

in Hamburg

---

*Printing the name in larger types in the original likely alludes to the fortuitous literal meaning, Werck - Meister (organ master).

†Printed *gEsellen*; by omitting the lower case letter g, the reader translates *Gesellen* (fellows) into *Esel* (asses).

PREFACE

You, my dear father, have with care described the making
Of organs, thus the weal of churches undertaking.
While many like it, for the jealous it is hell;
The sycophant resents the truth you tell.
For in this book your truthfulness is well reflected,
As you relate the knowledge faithfully collected.
And should Sir Blockhead rage and ply his motives odd,
The truth remains, and still our fortress is our God.

This was set down in honor

of his dear father with filial

faithfulness by

Joh. Barth. Werckmeister

Court teacher in Quedlinburg

Much has been written on all arts but naught transpired
On building organs; hence Werckmeister was inspired
By one of his good spirits that the church he thus
Might aid and serve in spite of jealous Zoilus.

This has been caused to be

appended in honor of the author by

Heinrich Jacob Wilcke

Citizen and organ builder

in Halberstadt

xxvi

Chapter One.

TO proof and examine an organ it is necessary first to inspect every conceivable facet. Then one needs to consult one's ear and judgment, in order to determine with the utmost care not only the present appearance of quality workmanship but also long-term dependability with regard to climatic conditions.

Here a pertinent question must be raised: should an organist or an organ builder be entrusted with the examination of an organ, or should both together be commissioned? The answer is: while an organ builder may have better insight in technical and mechanical aspects of building procedures than an organist, he is also quite handicapped in judging another builder's work. First, owing to his own building philosophy and occasional prejudices, he is likely to criticize construction procedures different from, though possibly superior to, his own. Indeed, many builders adhere so strongly to their preconceived notions that they will not abandon them even when defeated by incontrovertible arguments. Secondly, jealousy and emotions sometimes run so high that one organ builder cannot bear the sight of another, let alone approve the other's work. It has been the frequent and common experience for such examination arrangements to result in nothing but jealousy and squabbles. The most important aspects were often overlooked; church officials ended up being totally confused; in short, no organ builder will tolerate having his organ examined by another builder. Therefore it has become common practice to have organ proofings conducted by organists. And since a meticulous organist is in the best position to anticipate how climatic changes might affect an organ, it is most prudent to engage intelligent and impartial organists only for organ examinations. Even though they are not expert mechanics, they will find most defects by thoroughly testing the organ with their ears. On the other hand, organ builders will quarrel about nothing and forget correcting even the most obvious defects. Indeed, some organ builders are so jealous of each other that they would gladly damage the other's instrument if opportunity offered. Only recently it has happened that one slashed another's

bellows. Prior to the examination one must carefully read the builder's contract.

One might begin an inspection by examining whether the housing
of bellows be so located as to withstand damage by rain, storm, snow,
exposure to the sun, dry air or excessive humidity and the like. One
must be particularly wary of locating bellows directly under a roof,
where — owing to constant solar heat — they are sure to crack and
become useless. The bellows also must be protected against vandalism, which unfortunately occurs frequently. One must also determine if the bellows are made of good wood; if they are well constructed; if they inflate far enough; if they move well, evenly, gently
and slowly without shaking or creaking so as to guarantee swift in-
take and good retention of wind. It is very useful to saturate interior
surfaces with glue, and it is very good to line and seal them with
horse veins[7] which are best fastened by glued wooden brads. The
bellows must be well leathered and tightly sealed everywhere; the
weighting should be carefully balanced; and it ought to allow for
easy treading. Occasionally, it happens that an organ builder even
fails to assess accurately the range of the treading motion. In one
case I found that, as a result, the levers moved so low as to heave up
the entire bellows.[8] Had this not been quickly corrected the bellows
would have been torn apart in no time. As insignificant as such a defect may appear, as great a damage can it inflict, as experience has
often taught. There can be no question as to the need for solid anchor-
ing of the bellows. They must not jut out too far lengthwise over
their base frame, lest they work themselves loose from the wind
trunk, creating the frequently encountered leaks. Almost every organ
builder has his own method of detail construction. If this be found
workable and durable, one must not thoughtlessly reject it, as often
happens. Often bellows descent too swiftly owing not so much to

---

[7]Jakob Adlung explains in his *Musica mechanica organoedi*, p. 42:
"Horse veins are either straps of horse skin or actual dried horse veins, leg
tendons or sinews. They are more durable than common leather which has
a tendency to crack."

[8]The single-fold bellows, then universally in use, was operated by a
lever attached to the top plate.

their own faulty [construction] as to leakage in the wind trunks
and chests. Occasionally one even encounters leakage at the pallets.

Chapter Two.

O NCE satisfied as to good bellows construction and even wind —
the latter can best be tested with a special instrument, the wind
gauge — one should inspect the pipe work for straight, spacious, or
[as the case may be] crowded placement. If pipes are mounted too
close together, various problems may arise, particularly with regard
to steady voicing. One should also watch out for overly thin pipe
walls, especially when the metal is inferior owing to high lead content. A pipe made of too thin metal can hardly be removed without
incurring damage and dents from manual touch.

Secondly, such a thin-walled pipe cannot produce as good and
pure a sound as one with sufficient wall strength, since its entire
body vibrates so much that it tends to buzz constantly. However,
not the pipe materials but the air column in the body which is set to
vibrating by the wind refraction at the upper lip, is supposed to produce the sound.

Thirdly, a thin-walled pipe body, particularly one made of metal
with high lead content, corrodes[9] more easily than a pipe with a
sturdier wall. For tuning purposes, pipe [rims] ought not to be bent
in or out nor be disfigured by flaps or cuts. Not only does this look
ugly, but such pipes rarely stay in tune, partly because of these bent
[rims] and partly owing to the body temperature transmitted by
handling them. Touching a pipe makes it go sharp; in cooling off it
goes flat again. Therefore, the tuning cone is more practical. Here
now is one sure way to spot a negligent and impatient builder. For

---

9I have translated as "corrodes" Werckmeister's wording: "the saltpeter
eats through . . . ." Most so-called corrosion is "tin pest". Tin and lead occasionally turn into a non-metallic white powder which looks somewhat like
saltpeter.

unless he has the patience required for a fine and gentle initial cone tuning, not much good can come of it, and one must suspect that his pipes would come apart at the soldered seams with the application of the cone; thus, one may further conclude that the chest and the rest of his work may be of similarly shoddy quality.

Chimney flutes have to be well scaled;[10] open pipes should be perfectly round at the rims; caps of stopped ranks must fit snugly and tightly lest they gradually slip and cause pitch alterations.

Some people do not think very highly of partially stopped ranks such as the Rohrflöte [Chimney Flute]. They maintain that there is not much difference between it and a Gedackt. In fact, so many kinds of chimneyed flutes are now being built that they almost constitute a new stop family: *quidquid enim fieri potest per pauca, non debet plura* [at any rate, whatever is feasible in a few cases does not necessarily apply to more].

If one can see below the languid of an open pipe by about a hair's breadth, it is just right. If a stopped pipe chiffs,[11] its languid is usually a little too high, or else it may not yet have been cut up high enough. Here, experience is the best teacher.

Chapter Three.

PIPE feet must be checked for dents or [bleed] holes, as this may be indicative of [an attempted correction of] defective chest work. One must pay attention to open pipes uncharacteristically supplied with ears; this is an indication of things' being not quite right, betraying the master's laxity. Sometimes one comes across pipes inadequately soldered or having tiny sand holes[12] here and there that are hard to detect. These and other similar defects cause the pipe to

---

10Werckmeister seems to refer to a consistent "scale" curve formed by the chimney lengths.

11*Filpen* alternately connotes chiffing or overblowing.

12Some builders cast their metal on a sand-covered bench.

waver or speak improperly. Careless soldering of the languid is also quite common, causing pipes to cough and flutter, and then, our splendid organ maker is at a total loss as to what to do about this. Another great flaw is the failure to solder the languid exactly at a right angle or placing it too high or too low. In metal pipes, the languid may be adjusted for voicing purposes by bending it a little. One should also see to it that the edge of the languid is straight. If this is not the case, one may straighten it with a voicing knife.[13] In wooden pipes such flaws cannot be so corrected.

Large metal pipes must be given sturdy feet lest they settle and bend, so as to tilt sideways or even fall flat like drunken peasants, causing damage within the case. Therefore, it is not enough to rely on steadying large pipes in the pipe rack only; they must also be secured with a special hook at the top. How many beautiful organs have been neglected in this regard! One only needs to look at the organ in the famous castle church of Grüningen.[14]

Mixtures must be tested as to whether they yield the total effect promised by the contract. One may find pipes whose mouths have been pressed shut. For if they cannot voice and tune them purely enough, some organ builders, as a last but very bad resort, simply smother them, especially in multi-ranked mixtures with their great number of pipes.

Chapter Four.

ON examining reed stops, one should check for accurate proportional length and diameter of resonators within each rank. This is very important, for if the resonators of low pipes are very wide they are bound to out-shout the pipes in the treble range. It is a great shame that one rarely finds tonally balanced reed stops.

---

[13]This is not to be confused with nicking.

[14]See Werckmeister's *Organum Gruningense redivivum*, 1705; reprint Ed. Paul Smets, Mainz, 1932.

Occasionally this may be linked to such other causes as poorly computed resonator length, faulty wind, oblique attachment or variable width of reeds or shallots. The building of good and durable reed stops obviously requires great care. To facilitate easy tuning, the pipes must not be placed too close to each other. They must not be riddled with holes near the bottom, lest they give off childish sounds by comparison to their fellow pipes. They must be mounted securely. The boots ought to be wide enough to avoid contact with the tongues; otherwise one can never get them well tuned. Thick tongues are more durable than thin ones, but they require strong wind. The tuning wires must be adequately strong and [the holes through the block] should be so evenly drilled as to ensure smooth touch with the reed; neither should they be too feeble. They must easily yield to tuning and should sit neither too tightly nor so loosely as to drop down. Beaten[15] tuning wires drop through very easily, particularly if they are too thin to begin with.

It looks pleasant when the tuning wires are either identical, or when they increase or decrease proportionally in length. Brass wires are far better, as they do not rust [corrode] as easily as iron. Equally essential is the tight fitting of shallots and reeds. The shallots and tongues must be fitted within the blocks, the blocks also in the boots, lest they come off in tuning, something troublesome and annoying. Brass shallots are the most durable. Occasionally one finds them with soldered [organ] metal facing, intended to reduce the clattering of the tongue. Unless a reed stop is well manufactured it can quickly deteriorate in the hands of an inexperienced organist. The [shape, length and thickness] of the reeds must also be finely graduated according to their proportions.

At times, wooden blocks to which resonators and shallots are attached are set into tin or metal boots. For the most part, this is not advisable: if the wood shrinks, the wind dislodges the resonators [along with the blocks] which then end up being strewn all over the church; if the wood swells, it bursts the boots, notably those made of metal. This latter risk can be reduced by shaping the wooden

15Werckmeister's term *geschlagene Krücken* is ambiguous. Either he is referring to hammered as opposed to drawn or rolled wire, or he cautions against forceful application of the tuning knife.

block conically, pointing downward. But it is infinitely more advisable to join wood with wood, since woods will shrink and swell at the same rate; experience has shown such constructions to be durable and solid, particularly if identical wood is being used. Large shallots are customarily leathered so as not to rattle so fearsomely. It should be remembered, however, that tanned leather is preferable to tawed leather. The latter absorbs humidity which dissolves the glue so that it drops off, whereas tanned leather stays dry and retains the glue better. The large resonators for a 16′ Posaune are preferably made of wood rather than tin. For the thin tin rattles along quite strongly and ruins the tone quality, whereas wood, owing to its thickness, is not likely to rattle. A metal resonator is best when made thick enough.

Chapter Five.

THE wind chests will pass the test *quoad visum* [as far as visual appearance can indicate], if they are well constructed of high-quality, flawless and solid wood; and if the top boards are thick and strong, showing precisely bored and well-burned toe holes. Bearers (to either side of the slider) and sliders must be of identical wood and carefully matched,[16] otherwise the manipulation of stops may become very difficult with changes in the weather. Eventually, the sliders may break off altogether, requiring costly repairs. Therefore, it is very bad to use oaken sliders together with bearers of fir. Since fir shrinks more than oak in the dry season, the sliders will jam under the weight [of the top board], become difficult to move and may well break. In humid weather, however, they will move too easily, so as to allow runs.[17] Because fir swells more than oak in

---

[16]Werckmeister's wording *recht verkehret* means "alternated". It is reminiscent of Arnold Schlick's *verandert* (*Spiegel der Orgelmacher*, Chapter 9). Alternating the grain reduces warping.

[17]Werckmeister explains his distinction between run and cypher at the end of the chapter.

humid conditions, the bearers, in the process of expanding, will force the top board upward, away from [contact with] the sliders.

One should not agree to some pallets' having two or three springs while the rest have one. This is most annoying at the keyboard. For if one key is stiff and another light to the touch, it is impossible to play well, no matter how tonally beautiful the organ may be. Neither should one tolerate two kinds of springs for identical pallets, one strong and another weak, because this also causes all too familiar vexation at the keyboard. In this context it is very necessary to note that such pallets as are opened by stickers[18] should never be so installed as to be inaccessible. Whenever the weather changes or perhaps when a sticker is bent out of shape and binding, one must have easy access. For no matter how excellent and well-constructed an organ might otherwise be, the single defect of occasional ciphering would outweigh its good qualities; because of this shortcoming it would surely be criticized as useless; and it might, indeed, be totally unusable. On the other hand, if accessibility is provided to all places where cyphers are likely to originate, no real problem does exist. After all, wood will swell and shrink; therefore, one would hope that an organist, in case of emergency, would take the trouble to correct such defects. But many a careless organist is quick to seriously accuse the organ builder, making a mountain out of a molehill. Frequently, cyphers are traceable to the leather purse at the pull-down in the pallet box (particularly when the pallet box is made of fir). Wind seepage into the pallet apertures is caused by the swelling of the pallet box floor: The pull-downs are being dragged downward, especially when they are attached snugly without much play. Although this is easily remedied, not one out of ten knows why cyphering noises occur so frequently in humid weather. Most people blame it on warped pallets, which certainly is not always the cause of such hissing cyphers. Naturally, pallets ought to be made of good wood, strong enough to resist warping. They must be well leathered, not too scantily, so as to seal well. The leather should be warmed with the [hot] glue and attached smoothly and evenly. It is of utmost importance that the leathering of all parts assigned to sealing and containing wind hermetically be perfectly uniform. They ought

---

[18]Werckmeister refers to the stop pallets of the spring chest.

not to be thick in one spot and at another consisting of a patchwork of thinly cut strips glued on top of each other; nor should single pieces of leather be of variable thickness, especially not in chests. For no matter how accurately a chest or even a pallet might be planed flat, its precision would be marred by uneven leathering; it would necessarily produce runs. Therefore, an organ builder must always be sure to procure workable leather, evenly cut, and, in order to minimize hydrophilic properties, not too limy and nitrous. Most certainly, he should not, as has happened so often, ruin an organ by by stingily economizing in the purchase of high-quality leather. The inevitable result of perennial runs throughout the instrument's existence will only damage and destroy his reputation.

The generally incorrect usage of such often employed terms as run and cypher needs clarifying: cyphering connotes a clearly audible, full sound caused by a key's getting stuck or a valve's remaining open all the way; the term run should only be used in reference to furtive wind leakage from one channel to the other, or along a slider and elsewhere so that a neighbor pipe is affected.

The pallets must also be so placed as to allow for the necessary accessibility. Long pallets are preferable to wide and short pallets. The pallet springs must be sufficiently strong but not too hard [*i.e.* they must be resilient]. The guide pins between the pallets ought to leave enough play, lest the pallets bind and stick in humid weather; they should be straight, because they will get stuck if the pins are closer together near the grid surface; and they must not be too short, lest rapid motion result in the pallet's bouncing out from between the pins and coming to rest on the head of the pin; all this experience has verified.

The bungs must be strong and airtight, well leathered with well-heated glue, but they should not be glued shut as often happens. Rather they should be locked tightly with wedges so that the wind pressure cannot loosen them, particularly in the dry season. Access to the pallets is always essential.

Chapter Six.

WIND chest, wind trunk and bellows must be thoroughly glue-sized, otherwise the wind will sneak off through the pores unnoticed. One should also avoid patching and nailing. Screws, offering a reliable mode of fastening [wooden parts] in an organ, should be used wherever possible.

Occasionally, organ builders bore here and there in the chest little [bleed] holes going into the channels, either because the pallets seal unsatisfactorily or wind seeps from one to another channel or along the sliders. One also encounters such holes in the top board in proximity to the pipes. These holes will cause hissing cyphers when plugged up. In such cases, one must determine whether the defect originates with leaky pallets, or whether it is caused by wind seepage below the table, at the top boards or along the sliders.

One comes across quite a number of surreptitious tricks in the building trade. However, since such stopgaps often are more beneficial than damaging for a given organ, one cannot list them as unqualified faults under the heading "Defects." Indeed, some organ builders use tricks which not one out of hundred examiners will detect. Although it should not be condoned, such a minute loss of wind does not hurt an organ; as the saying goes, necessity does not discriminate. But it would be better if one were not bothered by Fontenelle,[19] hardship and wasp nests — I am unable to liken such defects to anything else. Some gentlemen of the building trade will undoubtedly have identified the targets at which I am aiming.

19Wordplay: fontanelle (covered opening; also ulcer) — Fontenelle (Bernard le Bovier de, 1657-1757, author of *Histoire des oracles*, 1686, in which criticism of pagan religions is slyly turned into a caustic critique of Christianity).

Chapter Seven.

THE action must be orderly and neatly constructed, and it should not be too crowded. Strong, pure wood must be used, particularly for the stop action rollers; if these are not sufficiently sturdy, the stops cannot be accurately manipulated. It is equally important that the pins [roller arms?] be sufficiently sturdy.

The roller boards need to be neatly designed. The rollers should be mounted neither too close to each other nor to the roller board, in order to avoid the abominable cyphering which results from the swelling of the wood in humid weather or from dirt. Therefore, it is not a bad idea to use horizontal [?][20] wood for the roller boards, or to mount the Rückpositiv rollers underneath [the board] in order to minimize dust interference.

Some builders eliminate the roller board, mounting the rollers instead on a strong oaken frame; this seems to have the additional advantage of more permanent key alignment. Others attempt to do without rollers, relying on squares only [i.e. fanning]. Still others experiment with a turned-around placement of the roller board, whereby the rollers are mounted front to back [?]. They claim that this arrangement results in more dependable key alignment, so that not one key rests higher than another [in the key bed]. In reality, however, this construction is rather perilous; for unless there is ample play, the roller pins will bind so badly with wood shrinkage that all keys stick. In order not to run such risks, it is best to retain conventional roller board construction. If the [trackers to the] keyboards are equipped with adjusting screws, they can be constantly maintained in good regulation.

The longer rollers must be sufficiently sturdy to escape torsion and bending, which adversely affect the playability of a keyboard.

---

[20]Werckmeister's vague term *gesetzt* could also mean "sectional" (from *Gesätz*), *i.e.*, constructed of separate beams rather than of one board. Adlung (*op. cit.*, Vol. II, p. 34), incorporating *verbatim* (and without acknowledging his source) almost the entire Chapter 7 of *Orgelprobe* into his treatise, does not attempt any clarification.

Heavy action or excessive depths of touch can be alleviated, first by giving mechanical advantage at the pallet connections [*i.e.* pull-downs], then at the roller arms, and then also at the point of connection with the key, which requires equally careful treatment. The roller arms should feature some adjustment device. For example, it might not be unfeasible to equip them with two or three holes to enable one the better to give or take [*i.e.* to adjust the ratio in the tracker hookup]. Incidentally, it should be remembered that the roller studs as well as the roller arms are best made of wood, since they do not clatter as much as iron ones. But even in the wooden studs the holes should not be so big as to allow for too much play; otherwise, the resultant rattling would have to be checked again by pounding little iron brads close to each moving pin [in order to reduce the excessive play].

The stops must be easily manipulable, not too hard nor too light; they should not over-pull [*i.e.* move the slider past the point of precise matching of slider and toe holes]; they must also be orderly arranged and quickly and comfortably accessible.

The stop irons in the Rückpositiv should be just as sturdy [as those of the other divisions]; for if they bend, they are adversely affected with regard to complete engagement or cancellation; this is a great nuisance, because then the division will rarely produce clean sound.

Chapter Eight.

IN view of my frequent references to the wind chest, and on the assumption that some amateurs or aspiring organists might be unacquainted with the meaning of this or that term or designation, I have decided to supply a brief description of a wind chest for the purpose of better comprehensibility (even though organ builders cannot seem to agree on a common terminology). The wind chest is a frame of oak wood, approximately three or four fingerbreadths high.

It is partitioned by inset, shank-like oak strips [bars] into as many compartments or channels as a given division [*Werk*] has keys. The relative size of a division, *i.e.* the projected number of stops, determines the exact dimensions of these channels.

The ancients used instead of a frame a strong oaken plank sizeable enough to accommodate the projected organ. They drilled the channels and, upon completed finishing, plugged them at either end; hence the term *drilled chests*. Others used inserts [*i.e.* ceilings] to seal chiseled channels; these they called bunged chests.[21] All channels of chests employing the aforementioned frame construction are tightly bunged underneath, usually by more than half [their length]. Then, the pallet box is attached under the remaining openings. It houses the main pallets[22] which cover the apertures in the channel floors; they open when their corresponding manual keys are depressed. On top of this frame — by now [*i.e.* at this stage of construction] it is already a wind chest — a board of approximately ½″ or ⅔″[23] thickness, called a table, is fitted and securely fastened. Then again, some builders do not use a table, preferring to plug the top of the channels with bungs. Sometimes, these are rabbeted into the bars, sometimes not. At any rate, the height of the frame must then be increased, lest the channels turn out too low and small, particularly in large organs. On top of the table or [as the case may be] of the bungs, which should be lined with leather, the bearers are fastened and the sliders adjusted [between them]. Also approximately ½″ thick, they run lengthwise with the chest.

Then holes are drilled through the sliders and the table or the bungs down into the channels. The wooden strips running parallel to either side of the sliders are called bearers. Right above these sliders

---

[21]*gespündete Laden.* Normally this term refers to a grid-type slider chest employing channel bungs instead of the table.

[22]Werckmeister introduces the term "main" (key) pallet, apparently to avoid confusion with the (stop) pallets in his discussion at the end of this chapter of the spring chest.

[23]According to D.-R. Moser, Werckmeister used the Rhenish *Zoll* and the Braunschweig *Elle*: 1 inch (*Zoll*) ca. 2.3 cm; 1 degree = 1/10 inch, ca. 2.3 mm; 1 yard (*Elle*) ca. 56 cm; 12 Rhenish *Zoll* approximately ½ Braunschweig *Elle*. All references to weights and measures in this translation represent Werckmeister's, *i.e.* unconverted, units.

and bearers the top boards, approximately 1½″ thick, are placed. They have to be very carefully fitted so that not the least bit of wind can escape anywhere or leak from one key [channel] to the next; but the sliders need to be easily moveable, so as to slide freely into "on" and "off" position, matching or blocking respectively their holes and those in the table or channel ceilings; hence the term *slider chest*. On this top board the pipes are mounted; its holes must exactly match those of the slider in "on" position. The underside of the top board is lined. The wind may be fed through the top board in a straight or oblique direction.[24] Above the top board is the pipe rack, which supports the pipes in upright position. It would be very helpful if pipe racks were furnished with holes [large enough] to reach through with a screwdriver in order to tighten or loosen all screws fastening the top board to the chest. For with variable weather, particularly during the fasting season,[25] the sliders become hard to move, at times they even break or jam completely. Therefore, this would be a good way to prevent many a mishap, not to speak of the costs incurred by the otherwise inevitable necessity of removing the entire pipe work. In this context I should also note that nowadays chests are no longer equipped with tables, which have a record of troublesome performance. The most distinguished builders prefer to rabbet the bungs [into the frame], therefore they have discontinued the [construction of wind chests with] tables.[26] This concludes the general discussion of slider chests.

In the spring chest each key [channel] has its own top board, and each pipe on that board has its own [stop] pallet. That means that there have to be as many pallets as there are pipes, excepting mixtures and other compound stops, where each chorus [*i.e.* the con-

---

[24]That is to say, the terminal points of the bore at the bottom and top sides of the top board respectively need not be perpendicular; "oblique direction" of the bore is indicated when slider and toe holes are not vertically aligned.

[25]"Fasting season," likely referring to Lent only, *i.e.*, the seasonal change from winter to spring; Werckmeister probably did not have in mind the mid-winter penitential season of Advent.

[26]Since the late eighteenth century, table constructions have gradually become the norm.

stituent pipes of one key] has one pallet. These top boards are set
directly onto the channels [since neither bearers nor sliders are re-
quired]. Each pallet is provided with a sticker. By means of these
stickers [all] the pallets [of one stop] are opened, as the stop beam
[mounted over each row of stickers] traversing the chest lengthwise
is lowered, when the stop is drawn. Upon cancellation of the stop,
the spring-loaded pallets automatically spring back into place, hence
the term spring chest. The pipes are mounted on the top boards in
the same manner as has already been described for the slider chest.
The pipe rack supporting the pipes to keep them from leaning is
known by many different designations among organ builders. For the
sake of brevity I shall not list them, just as I would prefer to bypass
some other terms on which organ builders cannot seem to agree, as
I have indicated earlier. I have confined myself to touching incidentally upon some basic terminology for the benefit of the beginner. An
amateur curious enough might wish to do some research of his own
to see for himself how well certain designations fit their objects. The
important thing for an organ is to be a good instrument; the terminology is of no essential significance.

Chapter Nine.

SOME people insist on mathematically investigating the pipes with
a little measure. However, I do not consider this necessary, since
organ builders should not use geometrically proportional scaling.
They are accustomed to slightly holding in the pipe width [diameter
?] for the bass range and large pipes and, conversely, to expanding
somewhat that of the smaller pipes, while at the same time adjusting
the pipe length, now expanding, now (but only by very little) re-
ducing it. Every organ builder applies his own special formula. Moreover, a given temperament affects the pipe dimensions as well. Generally speaking, the best effect is derived from a scaling pattern which,
in keeping with a geometrically proportional scheme, is relatively

wide in the *sonis gravioribus* [grave region], in large pipes and low-pitched ranks; and rather more narrow in *sonis acutioribus* [acute region] and in higher-pitched stops. The latter sounds lovely and bright, the former splendid and solemn.[27] Of course, consistent with the requirements characteristic of each stop, an overall balance should be maintained so that high-pitched pipes are not overpowered by the lower pipes. For the examination of other aspects [of pipe design], however, one might wish to use a measure.

The key [action] must feel to the touch neither too hard, lazy and wind-viscous [*windzäh*, *i.e.*, sluggish or having too much pluck], nor so light as to be disposed to cyphering. The keys must not lie so close together as to stick in humid weather. Neither pedal nor manual should clatter and rattle as this is a disgraceful thing and not to be tolerated. If the pedalboard and the manual are not carefully so placed that d in the pedal lines up perpendicularly with d′ sharp in the manual, or pedal c with manual c′ sharp,[28] one cannot play cleanly, unless one becomes used to it. It would be helpful, therefore, if organ builders could reach consensus in this matter. The most comfortable solution would be uniform alignments of the centers of pedal and keyboards.

---

[27]*Gravitatisch* as a descriptive term in seventeenth- and eighteenth-century organistic parlance, connotes not one single characteristic but a composite of qualities, such as: well-developed bass sound, majestic, dignified, noble, commanding respect, profound, solemn.

[28]Werckmeister's pitch designations are obviously erroneous; his text reads, . . . "so placed that the unlined d [*ungestricken*] in the pedal lines up perpendicularly with the D sharp in the manual, or pedal c with the manual c sharp." — In this translation the octaves are designated as follows: C c c′ c″ c‴.

Chapter Ten.

FOR the purpose of discovering by ear all that cannot be examined with the eye, one cancels all stops of the organ, but opens all pallets, not only those with legitimate but possibly also some with surreptitious functions: while the bellows are being operated in proper fashion, one places a plank across the entire pedal board and steps on it so that all or most pedal keys are depressed. If one then can hear [wind] blustering, rushing and running, all things are not well. Such a defect is usually related to the stop action. For unless the sliders have been reliably engineered, the full force of the wind lifts them up, and the wind penetrates around them into the holes and pipes. The same test is applied to the manuals by placing both arms on the keyboard. If an organ builder indicates displeasure with this procedure, one must pay particular attention to ensure that the bellows are actually being operated while all pallets are open. For some organ builders install secret valves to be opened or closed at the right moment, so that for the duration of this test no wind is admitted to the wind chest. In order to detect this [cheating] one need only draw a stop now and then [during the test]. Honest people, however, will not act so slyly. If the wind drop and the blustering is not too noticeable, one may let it pass, particularly if the weather has been dry. For it could not be otherwise, since sliders do shrink; that is, in a manner of speaking, a congenital characteristic of the slider chest. However, the limits of tolerating this defect are reached when — all stops having been canceled, the manual keys being depressed with both arms — the wind drop is so extensive as to cause the bellows to shake. In order to determine this [toleration limit], one of the examiners must test the keyboard by tapping [the keys] with both arms in quick succession, while the other observes the bellows. If these are shaking, there can be no doubt that the wind is allowed miraculously to escape, that holes have been drilled all over the top boards and the pipes, and that toes have been mashed. Some organ builders have so masterfully developed such practices that not one out of a hundred organists will detect these defects.

Special attention must also be given to close correspondence of the holes in the chest, top boards and sliders. It may happen that some pipes speak prematurely when a stop is being drawn very slowly. By the time the slider is fully drawn, these pipes will not receive enough wind, since [their holes] have been overpulled.

Chapter Eleven.

THE next step is to listen to one stop at a time, note by note, through the entire keyboard in order to determine if the pipes sound pure in themselves, if they have been evenly voiced, and if they speak promptly and accurately.

One must remember, however, that brightly voiced pipes cannot speak quite so instantly, particularly large open pipes of narrow scale. Of course, they can be voiced to speak more quickly, but [then] they also sound dull and unfriendly. It is better for a pipe to speak a little more slowly in return for retaining its brightness than to be cut up too high and dulled. Indeed, bright pipe sound is a virtue. One can always cut them up too high and dull them, but their former brightness cannot so easily be restored. Some voicers bend the [upper] lip outward to achieve quicker speech. But pipes [so voiced] overblow easily, do not stay in tune too well nor yield bright sound. However, everyone has to deal with this according to his taste. Next, one should listen to whether one pipe sounds bright and another dull, a defect which occasionally can also be caused by variable channelling in the top boards. But if one pipe speaks brightly and another sounds dull, the cause of the dull speech is too high a cut-up. Another check is to listen if perhaps the *Vicinus* [neighbor pipe] ghosts along (a point briefly raised earlier), which is an indication that the channels have cracks or holes or that the top board and the sliders in the chest are so poorly planed [straight] that the wind can go wherever it pleases. It is a bad business when this or that [unsolicited] pipe murmurs audibly along with playing, [particularly] in chordal [textures]. This is to be tolerated under no circumstances.

To be sure, this and similar defects can be alleviated to a certain extent by bleed holes in chest and pipes, as I have mentioned earlier; but it is a deplorable practice. Throughout its lifetime nothing good can be expected of such an organ. Another matter to be tested by ear is good ensemble quality[29] of an instrument. Next, one should turn to the Principal 4' or Octave 4', to which the organ builder tunes [the remaining stops]. One has to listen to whether this is tuned accurately, how the temperament is set and if it is so devised as to be of bearable quality. For one comes often across organs that are tempered in such a manner that some fifths are so impure as to be totally useless. Obviously, it then becomes necessary to correct this *Vitium* [deficiency]. After this, one listens to whether all octaves are tuned pure within this same 4' stop; then, one checks out all stops of the organ, one at a time and key by key, together with this 4' Principal or whatever stop the builder has used as [tuning] stop in order to determine if all stops are in tune with it. Particular attention is to be given to the mixtures, especially also to whether all pipes belonding to a given key do speak and live up to their obligations. In this regard, fraudulent practice abounds. As mentioned earlier, some organ builders list in their specifications mixtures of eight, ten, and twelve ranks, whereas in reality hardly three or four pipes produce a decent sound.

29Werckmeister's term *Chormässig* could also be interpreted as "adhering to *Chorton*" (as opposed to *Kammerton*). Accordingly, he might refer to tuning-pitch level rather than ensemble blend.

Chapter Twelve.

HAVING tested the stops individually, one proceeds by listening to them in pairs, being careful to note if some clash together;[30] then in groups of three, four, etc., following the same testing procedures. One must establish if they sound well together in chordal [textures]; if they sound pure; if they rob one another of wind; if they suffer from wind deficiency, a frequent byproduct of too-small wind ducts, channels or pallets.

N. B. [*i.e. nota bene*, note well]: This *Vitium* [deficiency] was called consumption [*Windseichte*] by some ancients. Even today some people feel that it is curable by supplying an organ with some additional bellows. But they do not understand the nature of wind. One single bellows must be capable of producing adequate wind, provided that channels, pallets and wind inflow[31] are constructed just right and in appropriate dimensions. For it often happens that the channels are built too small. If furthermore they do not have enough depth [*i.e.* capacity], and if, in addition, the pallets are too short, the pipe work, particularly with full organ,[32] cannot possibly receive sufficient wind. This *Vitium* [deficiency] is rather common in old organs. Therefore, such a defect must be considered especially in the instance of a renovation. Otherwise, all efforts will be for naught, and a consumptive organ it shall remain.

One should also listen to whether the pipes drop in pitch or lose in brightness when one sustains a full chord, and whether they rise again or sound even duller with the next treading of the bellows. This defect has various causes, but most of the time it is linked to a poor design of bellows and wind supply. For if the outflow of wind

---

30Literally, "if some stand together." Werckmeister might either refer to a tuning differential causing beats or to too-close mounting of pipes causing acoustic interference patterns.

31The old German terms *Zufall* and *Einfall* refer to volume rather than to pressure.

32Werckmeister's term *im vollen Werke* most likely denotes divisional principal *plena* with and without reeds.

from the several bellows is insufficient or if the [check] valves between the bellows and the wind trunk are too small, no single bellows
can contribute enough wind for full organ. Therefore (even though
one, two or three stops, together may sound pure) clean intonation
cannot be maintained with full organ. Such deficiencies of wind must
necessarily be corrected; otherwise an organ builder can never tune
cleanly, and the organ will not be in tune throughout its existence.
Reed stops together with full organ would stay even less in tune.
This fault can often also be encountered, when bellows lift too high
and have no counterweights [*gegengewichte*].

Some organs run on insufficient wind because of [intentionally
light] weighting of the bellows. For if some organ builders were to
provide their instruments with somewhat aggressive wind, it would
soon betray their negligence in the [construction of the] wind chests;
these would hiss here and cipher there. One should also listen for
gulping and wind shaking, or for all too strong and unpleasant
tremores [trembling] in sustained right-hand [chords] when the left
hand or pedal engages in passage work.

This is a very common *Vitium* [deficiency] varying in extent
from organ to organ. There are also various opinions as to its causes.
But the main cause is this: When too much wind is being used
[literally, "when the outflow of wind is altogether too great"],
shaking necessarily will occur upon hasty closing of a pallet: the
wind [owing to the bellows' momentum generated by the rate of
wind consumption] bumps into the pipes from bouncing bellows. One
can notice this by playing continuously repeated full-chord patterns
in low ranges: whenever the motion of the key [action] coincides
with that of the bellows,[33] they are set to [frantically] playing and,
deflating rapidly, they push the wind with considerable force into the
pipes. Thus, no [wind] steadiness can be achieved on such an organ,
indeed, it [*i.e.* the wind or the pipe speech] falters altogether in these
repeated-chord patterns. Since the shaking produces lapses and re-
cession of wind, the wind supply in the pallet box cannot satisfy the
[demand from the] rapidly functioning main pallets. Regarding this
[problem], I have recently seen [the construction] of an eminent

---

[33]Werckmeister is describing testing the bounce frequency of the wind
system.

organ builder, which first collects the wind from all bellows in one spacious wind trunk. From this channel, individual wind ducts connect with each wind chest, thus the wind is steady. If, however, a wind duct is branched off from another which in itself is hardly sufficient for one wind chest, trembling and unsteadiness are inevitable. Another cause for unsteadiness is [too] small [check] valves between bellows and wind ducts. For if the wind duct is not served adequately by the valve, more wind is consumed than can be supplied it. Therefore, the valves must be fashioned somewhat large, but rather more wide than elongate and trimmed down at the bottom, lest they tremble or rock with their own weight.

Others attribute the main cause of unsteady wind to very short and wide pallets, maintaining that their hasty shutting action causes wind shaking. However, wide pallets are rather more responsible for hard key action with much pluck. The wind presses against the wide [surfaces of the pallets] and offers considerable resistance to them. If, on the other hand, a pallet is long and slender, not wide but tall and sharp-edged, it opens more easily and shuts more gently.[34] According to some opinions, wind shaking might be avoided by wind ducts that are kept more narrow at the pallet box than back [at the bellows]. Unsteadiness of wind would thus be eliminated, because reconveyence of wind shaking through the duct would be counteracted by renewed wind pressure from the bellows. The longer a wind duct, the slower the ebb and flow of wind. Still others are of the opinion that large [tone] channels can also be the cause of wind shaking, since [relatively] strong inflow is required to fill up such large cavities.

Although all of the conditions here listed may be contributing factors [to wind shaking], I stand by my claiming extensive wind drop as the main cause. There are a number of additional, incidental conditions which for reasons of sheer lengthiness cannot here be mentioned. Every thinking organ builder will take all these into account.

---

[34]Werckmeister seems to refer to a pallet shape essentially triangular in section.

Chapter Thirteen.

IT is also necessary to play through one stop after another in major thirds. For it is well known that often when a third is played on a slider chest, the middle key is also heard. For example, when C and E, mounted near each other in one of the case towers, [are played], D which is mounted between them is also heard. Some have called this the *wolf* in the organ. But this is not a genuine wolf; this *Vitium* [fault] usually derives from the slider. If the wind can push the slider upward, it will gain enough access to the pipe mounted between C and D. Another cause could be wind leakage from one channel to another. In this case, the run is common to all stops [on that chest].

The wolf, on the other hand, may also be caused by poorly tuned and scaled pipework. Namely, when two pipes forming a consonant [interval] and sounding pure in themselves are played together, a third, slightly dissonant sound, *i.e.* a combination tone, might be perceived. This sound is not generated within another [a third] pipe. Rather, it is the two pipes [sounding together and] intended as consonance that cause this dissonance because of poorly designed bodies, [mutually] heterogeneous scaling in width and capacity, and poor tuning and voicing.

There is no other remedy for this than cutting open one of the two pipes to either narrow the scale of the one or widen that of the other, or else to revoice; only then can a pure consonance be obtained. Such and similar mathematical and physical pranks often come to pass in organs and many people are at a loss as to correcting such a *Vitium* [fault]. Indeed, many will swear to one faulty pipe's being the cause of this kind of dissonance; of course it will prove to be otherwise.

Still other things happen. For example, tune c absolutely beatless to c', then tune the upper octave c" to c'; even though c'-c and c'-c" sound clean, yet c-c" remains quite impure. The cause for this might best be illustrated with a parable: If one allows two lines to converge onto a dot from opposite directions, they each will have reached and joined up with the dot as their intended goal. However, since their respective points of contact are peripheral, they are not yet mutually joined together, but must first touch each other, figuratively speaking, in the center of the dot in order to be merged together; the same applies to the tuning. If the pipes are large, one must imagine a spacious dot, but aim for dead center. It is well known that at the point where a pipe starts to be in tune with the other, it can still be coned in or out a good deal, staying in tune all the while. However, if one keeps on coning, the dot will [eventually] be traversed, in a manner of speaking, and the pipe once again goes out of tune. The same [phenomenon] explains the following: if one tunes separately two keys of a mixture to two corresponding principal pipes sounding a beatless octave, each of the mixture keys will be clean in itself; but if one plays the two mixture keys together, they sound badly out of tune, because the center of the dot has not been hit by this tuning [procedure]. Another frequent cause for an organ's sounding out of tune is poor pipe scaling. Then, with climatic changes, the pipes distone and go out of tune. Bad tuning also can stem from great haste on the part of the organ builders, when they do not allow the pipes to cool off. For pipes which were in tune while warm[35] will go out of tune in cooling off. Then again, when metal pipes show marked differences in wall thickness, as often happens, the thinner pipes cool off faster than those with stronger walls. One must watch out for all these things. Seldom will one find an organ where all keyboards are in tune from octave to octave, particularly the mixtures; this failing is not praiseworthy. Wooden pipes, especially if they have relatively thick walls, cool off even more slowly than metal pipes. It is therefore well nigh impossible for all stops to stay in tune with one another. At any rate, I have not ever observed that much patience in organ builders, nor have I ever heard an organ where all stops were in tune when checked against each other. Nevertheless, it is possible and can be achieved by diligent and special effort.

35Not only the touch of a hand but also cone tuning generates some heat.

Chapter Fourteen.

THE wider the scale of a Subbass the more pompous and full it sounds. By nature, open 16' basses cannot speak quite as quickly as stopped pipes. An Untersatz, particularly one of 16' [pitch], must speak audibly and clearly, no one pipe sounding stronger than another. Therefore, the wind inflow for the large pipes of the Subbasses must be sufficient, otherwise not much good can be expected. High wind pressure in itself is not enough; it must be coupled with sufficient inflow. However, it often happens that a pipe [as heard] from the key desk may sound quite soft and appear to be voiced rather dull. But elsewhere [in the room] it sounds as strong as the other pipes, possibly even stronger. Therefore, an examiner must listen extensively before reaching his verdict. It might be that the pipe appears dull sounding because of awkward acoustic conditions pertaining to a particular point or angle in the room. In fact, a pipe will sound stronger in one spot of a room than in another; even one pace can make a difference. Therefore, one must not pass judgment on overall evenness [of organ sound] from just one location [within the room]. Change in weather conditions usually brings with it slight alterations of the pipes. For in the winter, when the air is denser,[36] the pipes drop in pitch, whereas they rise in the summer. In this process, some pipes occasionally get lost in tuning [*i.e.* they may not sharp or flat uniformly with the rest of the flue chorus]. These the organist must note, and the organ builder must rectify the situation before the warranty expires, along with any other defects that [may] have surfaced and have been duly noted by the appointed organist during the year of warranty.

I shall not discuss scaling, as I have already been accused of merely abetting the bunglers in this little book. I have already answered these charges, though, by stating that all organ builders who

---

[36] Werckmeister's term *dicke Luft* apparently refers to the higher humidity typical of European summers. He is in error in ascribing the pitch differences to humidity and not temperature.

indulge in inferior workmanship and who do not benefit the churches by dint of dependable work are bunglers. This little book was written for the specific purpose to do away, once and for all, with bunglers' work; no one should attempt to teach himself from this book how to build an organ. For in this little treatise I have not described how an organ should be built, but how it should be proofed after it has been built. Hence, my discussion of the wind chest was also bound to be rather unspecific in the absence of exact data as to number and kind of stops for a projected organ. Only [on the basis of these data] can one supply exact specifications as to the size of wind chest components. For additional intelligent study and information one might read Bendeler's *Organopoia* [*sic*; Johann Philipp Bendeler, *Organopoeia oder Unterweisung, wie eine Orgel . . . zu erbauen*, printed ca. 1690 in Quedlinburg]; further contemplation is bound to advance one's understanding. But it is always advisable, for various reasons, to provide for more wind inflow than is indicated by mathematical computation.

Some organ builders turn scaling into lengthy and grand procedures; some guard it as their most precious secret, only because they wish to aggrandize themselves by it. If one takes a closer look at it [*i.e.* scaling], it turns out to be about as difficult an art as the egg of Columbus.[37] To be sure, [scaling] is quite important; but an organ builder ought not to be so [secretively] possessive about it toward his journeymen and pupils as to leave them confused. Without wishing to brag about it, I could relate various scaling procedures in the simplest terms. But since this is neither my business nor my stated intention I shall desist. The main purpose of scaling rests on [the premise] that the large pipes in the bass range cannot be given width measurements according to musical proportions [*i.e.* halving at octave]. Rather, one must always subtract a little from the width in order to achieve balanced sound, so that the tall pipes do not out-

---

[37]"The egg of Columbus" connotes a simple solution to a seemingly difficult problem. An originally Spanish idiom, *huevo del Juanelo*, has little John find the simple solution of crushing one end of an egg to the problem of making it stand upright. Among various historical personalities to have been credited with this feat, Columbus supposedly performed this trick at a banquet given in his honor by Cardinal Mendoza in 1493 (according to Benzoni's 1565 *Historia del mondo nuovo*).

shout the small pipes, a fault that one finds in many organs. The real *Arcanum*,[38] to be arrived at both mathematically and mechanically, is the determination of how much to subtract from the tall and give to the small pipes. And even though one cannot strictly apply theoretical proportions to the absolute relationship between length and width, they nevertheless remain the true basis for [the practice of] scaling. For whatever is subtracted from the width of the pipe body must be added to its length, not by the exact but by a proportionally lesser amount. This seems paradox, yet it is a real truth.

The rule according to which the cut-up must be one third of the mouth width is not [to be interpreted as a] universal [law], for a wide pipe does not require such a high cut-up as a narrow pipe. Furtherwore, wind pressure differs from organ to organ, likewise one organ builder employs [relatively] wide, another [relatively] narrow scaling.

It is also very important that the stops one must use for ensembles be designed and scaled according to a common plan. For example, c′ of Principal 8′ must correspond in scaling to c of Octave 4′. The latter must also be identical in scale to F of the Quint 3′ [*i.e.* 2⅔′] and to C of Octave 2′. In this manner, all pipes should retain consistency of scaling, even the mixtures, otherwise no organ can be tuned cleanly. Even if one should succeed in tuning it, it will change with the weather. For a wide pipe will soon miss the pure air, will rebel and become hostile to the narrow-scaled pipes. Wide-scaled stopped ranks are very good for large congregations as they are capable of filling a church. A wide Gedackt 8′ can be more effective than a narrow Principal 8′, particularly with full organ.

---

[38] *Arcanum* is the alchemical term for the mysterious substance believed to be capable of changing base metals into gold.

Chapter Fifteen.

A REED stop must have quite uniform tone color. It should not happen that within the same stop one pipe sounds like a common Regal, the second like a Trumpet, the third like a Dulzian, the fourth like a Schalmei. Each stop and pipe must sound according to its assigned characteristic and project its intended tone color. Much depends on well proportioned resonator dimensions. One can actually observe nature playing her little game in the resonators, as she refuses to accept and tolerate alien sounds that defy conformity. For example, an 8′ [reed] pipe pitched c will speak with any other resonator producing identical pitch attached to its block and shallot, and also with the resonators of g and c′ pipes: if one were to try the same with the resonator of an f-sharp pipe [inserted in a c-pipe boot], for example, one could not induce the c pipe to sound. Thus, one can see how proportionally related sounds will work together.

Each reed pipe must attack easily and speak accurately without too much rattling, fluttering or shrilling; the low pipes ought not to outshout the others. The preconditions for tonal balance in reed stops are not only good dimensions of reeds and shallots, as has previously been mentioned, but, most importantly, good proportional scaling [of resonators] with regard to diameters as well as to length. Failing these, neither tonal balance nor [good] tuning can be achieved; the pipes cannot be regulated, because the capacity of the resonators is so totally disproportionate to the [intended] tonal characteristics that no similarity can be attained. That is the reason why some organ builders pierce holes into the resonators or the boots, thereby inflicting uneven loudness on the stop. It has also previously been mentioned that the low pipes of long scale [i.e. full-length resonators], such as Posaune, Trumpet, Schalmei should not outshout the small pipes. Therefore, the organ builder must most of all be careful to avoid too wide resonators in the bass range. For this is the main factor of loudness in [reed] sound. The treble range of reed stops, on the other hand, will do well with wider [resonators], as it does sound good when endowed with some pervasive bite. Organ builders play perhaps the wrong tune, when their reeds are overly bragging in the bass range yet step quite softly in the treble, so that one can hear little of the smaller and treble pipes.

When one uses one of these [*i.e.* low reed stops with overly wide, full-length resonators] all by itself, it sounds as though trombones or trumpets were being played together with Cytharinas [small lutes]. The use of the tremulant will not be detrimental to a well made reed stop. If it cannot stand it [the tremulant], it is of little use. I can state with certainty that a good reed stop will neither incur detrimental effects nor go out of tune when the tremulant is used, unless a tremulant were to beat all too dreadfully.

Chapter Sixteen.

THE tremulant must beat very gently and must steadily maintain the speed to which it is set, even with big registrations. It must not dampen the [sound of] a division into sluggish or even sour intonation, a common condition [in organs] where the tremulant is placed into the wind trunk. The speed of the tremulant is a matter of personal taste; as the saying goes, *quod capita tot sensus* [there are as many preferences as there are minds]. The main concern should be steadiness of beating. The least commendable feature of a tremulant is rattling and hissing, audible throughout the church. All tremulants must be hidden from view, lest one or the other [of the parishioners] be incited to laughter on seeing it in operation, causing thereby a public offense in the church. All couplers must be reliably and durably constructed, lest they be detrimental to the organ by causing ciphering. The wires must not be too weak so as to eliminate the need for constant bending and curving [by way of adjusting the mechanism]. All components must accurately and exactly mesh together. Even so, the weather factor is a source of so much trouble in this matter that some people want to eliminate couplers altogether. However, depending on quality workmanship some couplers are quite acceptable. Whenever possible, the bells of a Zimbelstern might be so selected as to afford a certain agreement with the organ — for example c-e-g-c' etc. They must sound and tinkle nicely and brightly, not like cowbells, as one occasionally encounters. The mechanism of the Zimbelstern must be nicely bushed lest it clatter too much.

Chapter Seventeen.

THE examiner has to play the instrument extensively, using a variety of [organistic] techniques, checking all the while by eye and ear if perhaps one or the other key might stick or any other troubles develop. Allowing some one or two hours for such a proofing is simply not enough. For how could one or two persons possible inspect in so short a time every facet of what a number of people could barely finish in one or two years. Obviously, one must examine everything in detail; one should also very thoroughly discuss with the organ builder why this or that has been done or omitted; and one must allow ample time for all phases [of the examination]. The organ builder might also be consulted as to how and where best to fix the organ (by way of anticipating this or that future malfunction), so that the organist might be in a position quickly and without damage to the organ to take care of such defects should the need arise. The foregoing is a brief account of basic eventualities in organ proofing with particular attention to the slider chest.

Turning our attention to spring chests, we might first point out that they are rarely being built because they require much more production time than slider chests. Secondly, few organ builders are familiar with them. Thirdly, they need careful maintenance, for one has to fuss with them constantly: now a sticker gets stuck; now the top boards shrink, or the wedges holding down the top boards come loose with dryness; a spring may jump out — something that happens very often; a sticker misses its pallet, or the pallet returns faultily, failing to seal completely; sometimes the sticker holes are unevenly drilled, in which case the stop beams beat [the stickers] totally out of shape; the stop beam rises too high [on cancellation of the stop], allowing (alas) the stickers to jump out; the springs may become so weak that the stickers bind and the pallets remain open; then again, springs may jump out all the way; at other times some [dirt] gets under the pallets; in short, a sophisticated construction requires frequent repairs. There is so much more work and fussy detail construction in the spring chest than in the slider chest that one can easily see why it requires more maintenance than a slider chest. For example, the stop pallets of the spring chest are often attached to the top boards with tinned sheet metal. Later, when the metal starts rusting, it also corrodes the leather [linings], and, once again, the gentlemen of the trade have found themselves a job; they profit by the loss which the church and congregation have suffered. Therefore, brass, not iron or sheet metal, should be used to attach the stop pallets. See also Praetorius [*op. cit.*], Vol. II, p. 197 ff; likewise p. 159 ff,[39] for this author's opinion on spring chests.

Chapter Eighteen.

SUCH a [spring] chest appears to be a fine invention, as indeed some people still claim. For provided it be diligently constructed, particularly as regards airtight yet easily accessible top boards, such an organ should never need a general overhaul, as long as it and its wood were to last; for one person could without much trouble remove one top board after another in order to correct any defect. This does appear most advantageous. However, if its longevity were in-

---

[39]In Chapter 12 (pp. 107-09), Praetorius, by way of a brief historical survey, summarizes differences of construction between spring chest and slider chest. He emphasizes the need of excellent workmanship for the former, but carefully avoids stating a preference for either. No specific reference to spring chest construction is contained in Chapter 4 (pp. 158-160).

deed so exceptional, would it then have been necessary nearly three hundred years ago to zealously develop the slider chest as a viable alternative, as Praetorius reports in the aforementioned passage? For the very reason that such spring chests are susceptible to troubles too numerous to be discussed here even briefly they are used by only very few builders. Particularly if they are shoddily constructed and [prove] to be inaccessible here and there, one may well expect from them over a thousand times more trouble than from slider chests, as experience has shown. One [type of] spring chest construction permits removing the top boards [containing the stop pallets] from under a fixed top board on which the pipes are mounted. But because this top board is rigidly affixed and cannot be adjusted by way of screws, it is inevitable that in dry weather wind will leak between [lower] and [upper] top boards, thus eluding the pipes. In the (hardly realistic) contingency of the [top board] wood's being so well seasoned as to be incapable of shrinkage, one would still have to anticipate its swelling in damp weather: not one of the [lower] top boards could be removed without demolishing the fastening [of the upper top board]. If, however, the top board on which the pipes are mounted were to be constructed so as to be adjustable by screws when the weather changes, the great advantage of this improvement would justify the increase in required man hours. It would allow for solving the problem [of swelling] should one develop. Still, should organists or organ builders be expected to spend their waking hours at the organ after each drastic change of weather? I think this would often be [conveniently] forgotten. Notwithstanding the argument advanced by some people that the easy access to the top boards for the purpose of minor adjustments eliminates the need for a general overhaul, experience teaches otherwise. Upon request I can furnish ample proof.

In view of the scarcity of spring chests and because of their sophistication, I prefer the slider chest, which is consistently durable provided it is well made to begin with. Experience attests to a well built slider chest's life expectancy as well exceeding a hundred years. An eminent and famous organ builder tells of his removing in 1694 a slider chest from [the organ] in St. Martin's Church of Gröningen which had been built by one Martin Agricola in 1442.[40] This chest he attested to be in such good condition as to promise serviceability for another hundred years. It had to be retired only because it featured too few keys to be useful in present-day musical practice. But there is no end to the need of tinkering with a spring chest. It almost necessitates employing on a regular basis an organ technician, something organ builders are quick to accept. And if they faithfully attend to an organ, they deserve such an arrangement. I for one wish to caution any one regarding spring chests, as I have come to know by experience their virtues.

Chapter Nineteen.

THE provision, fancied by some, of making one stop playable by itself in the pedal as well as in the manual [*i.e.* duplexing] is not advisable by and large. For experience has shown that it does not often succeed. Frequently it sounds sour, especially in the reeds, because of uneven wind inflow; or because the wind is hampered by top-board channelling; or because of discrepancies in the distance to the pipes.[41] Therefore it is preferable to give each stop its own slider, unless one can so design it [*i.e.* transmission] as to be reliably functioning; otherwise the entire construction is useless. Admittedly, it is a welcome *Compendium* [saving] for poor churches unable to afford many large ranks, since this [*i.e.* transmission] is usually ap-

---

40Most likely relying on (slightly inaccurate) memory, Werckmeister seems to refer to the renovation of this organ in 1691-92 by Arp Schnitger. Also, the builder of this chest was not Martin (1486-1556) but Rudolf Agricola (1444-86).

41Adlung, *op. cit.*, Vol. I, p. 193, cites literally this entire passage, but with the following comment: "Werckmeister deems it inadvisable to . . . . However, none of these defects need to be feared, if an organ builder proceeds with the necessary caution and precision."

plied to large stops. The so-called flutter valves[42] in spring chests also cause frequent trouble.

Good organ builders must carefully endow their wind systems with reliability and must unfailingly discover the causes for occasional unevenness of wind. For if the winding is faulty to the extent of variable inflows, no steady intonation can be achieved. Since unsteadiness of wind now and again is traceable to the bellows, that precision workmanship of an organ builder is most praiseworthy which achieves totally balanced and even wind. The bellows are so installed and constructed or, if necessary, equipped with weights that a varianve of wind [pressure] — measurable with the aid of the wind gauge (a special measuring device) — becomes visually observable by the adding to, or removing from, the larger bellows as little as one pound of weight. But some organ builders think they can ensure steady wind simply by ear, [haphazardly] adding or removing [to or from the upper plate of the bellows] some bricks. But they are way off the mark. An organist blessed with such an instrument will have his fill of troubles. For just when he thinks he has finally succeeded in tuning, for example, a reed pipe, it will change altogether in sound quality at the point of alternation between the deflating of one and the inflating of another bellows, or when the bellows may bind at the fold. Many such an organist would rather go threshing [grain], wishing that tuning belonged elsewhere [i.e. were not part of his profession]. In that manner many a reed stop has been ruined.

---

[42]Consistent with Werckmeister's definition of pallets at the end of Chapter 20, these flutter valves (probably identical with Praetorius' *Stoehnfedern*) are not to be confused with wind-trunk ventils (*Sperrventile*). Rather, they appear to be check valves in, or contiguous to, some individual channels for the purpose of preventing wind feed-backs ("short circuits") in transmissions.

Chapter Twenty.

MOST organ builders claim to be able to achieve even wind [pressure] without the benefit of a wind gauge,[43] asserting that all is well if the pump levers move equally. But I have found this to be deceptive [in the following practical experiment]: so long as three [of four] bellows were descending evenly, the wind [pressure] also was even. Adding the fourth to the other three bellows immediately resulted in the wind pressure's rising by several degrees. However that same bellows which increased the wind pressure did either descend more slowly or not at all when operated simultaneously with the others. Yet, when operated alone, it produced higher pressure. This difference [of wind pressure] resulted from this bellows' hard-opening valve: when all bellows were in operation, its valve was held shut causing the [fourth] bellows to cease movement. Increased weighting of the fourth bellows gives it the advantage [over the other three bellows; *i.e.* its valve now is enabled to overcome the resistance offered by the other bllows]; consequently the wind pressure increases by several degrees even beyond the earlier measurement. This proves that the valves must be carefully regulated so as to open and close neither too tardily nor too easily, lest they start fluttering. This defect [*i.e.* variance in wind pressure] would hardly have been detected without the aid of the wind gauge. Yet, someone might ask: how could the wind [pressure] vary if it emanates from one single, evenly-weighted bellows? Answer: the reason is quite apparent. The motion of a bellows describes in effect the arc of a circle. The closer it moves to the point where the weight is perpendicularly above the center [of this circle], the less [power] there is; the farther away [from dead center], the more.

Experience furthermore teaches that the bellows' [downward] movement will be noticeably impeded if the folds spread open too

---

[43]As shown on the frontispiece of *Orgelprobe*, and as described in Chapter 25, this seems to be Christian Foerner's *Windprobe*, invented ca. 1667. See also Adlung, *op. cit.*, Vol. II, p. 79f and the same author's *Anleitung zu der musikalischen Gelahrtheit*, Erfurt, 1758, pp. 363 and 542.

wide so that the planks[44] form too blunt an angle. One need only construct a bellows with two [instead of one] folds [to find the following]: just as the lower fold has fully collapsed and the upper fold begins collapsing, the wind gauge registers an additional drop and ensuing decrease in wind [pressure]. If one [by way of trying to avoid this] takes to deliberately curtailing the bellows' travel [*i.e.* using shallow but very fast treading], I shall have to answer: this is even worse, because the bellows run out [*i.e.* deflate] that much faster. As a result, the *Calcant* [operator of the bellows] is compelled to tread constantly, thereby causing [wind] trembling, especially in the summertime when the bellows run less economically because of the greater incidence of little cracks and slightly enlarged pores in the wood. And many an organist has painfully experienced the spasmodic and erratic unevenness which this frantic treading imparts to the wind. The organ builder, of course, once having gotten away [*i.e.* once the organ has been officially accepted], could not care less whatever might happen.

One means to encourage even wind production can be the slightly slanted mounting of the bellows so that the side with the wide fold is lower than the other. The exact degree of the slanting is best determined from the bellows' inflated position. Likewise, one can improve bellows that open too far with different types of counterweights. This latter method is unfeasible, however, for bellows with two or more folds, *Experto credas Ruperto* [you may trust Mr. Expert].

In view of my frequent references to valves and pallets, it may be useful for the beginner to acquire the information requisite to differentiating between them. In order to avoid confusion, I have decided to describe some of these here: first, there are the bellows [*i.e.* intake] valves admitting air to the bellows. Next, there are the wind trunk [*i.e.* exhaust] valves; located in the wind trunk where the bellows gives off the wind, they prevent mutual wind robbing between the several bellows. Thirdly, there are the main pallets, operated by the key action, which enable [the pipes to] sound. Then, there are in the spring chest the spring pallets [*i.e.* stop pallets] which are op-

---

[44]Werckmeister's term *Spoene* (archaic plural of *Span*, *i.e. Spanbalg*) as well as his description of the bellows' function clearly suggests single-fold bellows.

erated by means of the stop beam. There are as many stop pallets as there are pipes in a given chest — mixtures and composite stops excepted; there, some two, three, four or more pipes are served by one [such] pallet. Finally, one may also encounter special valves, by means of which the wind within the trunks can be blocked here and there, hence the term wind-trunk ventil [*Sperrventil*]. Concerning counterweights [on bellows] I wish to add that they are most useful. Yet, in my experience, the present-day single-fold bellows can be so accurately adjusted without counterweights as to eliminate wind drops of [as little as] one degree [see footnote 23], no matter how high they travel. The latter [incidentally] can be achieved with the horse veins, rather than with counterweights [by especially tight installation]. Such bellows thus have permanently built-in counterweighting regardless of their relative positioning. In any case, an organ builder must handle this matter very sensitively to avoid overcompensation by counterweights. Duple- or triple-fold bellows cannot be counterweighted. But then, they are no longer in use.

HERE FOLLOW SOME TIPS
Which might come in handy with respect to organ building and contracting.

Chapter Twenty-One.

REGARDING contracts I should like to suggest, that first of all, one should make some inquiries as to whether the organ builder with whom one is about to contract has a good reputation; whether he has previous experience; whether his instruments have held up well and have been favorably judged. One might also gather some information as to his performance as a journeyman, whether he is intelligent and has a good record as a quality worker. It is quite essential to consult a knowledgeable organist beforehand to ensure a good specification as well as attention to a number of important details. Actually, I should here furnish some sample specifications. But, since this could turn out to be too lengthy I confine myself to a few tips: Be sure to specify a Gedackt or Quintadena 8' for a small organ or Positiv of four, five or six stops. This [fundamental stop] allows for a variety of [musical] possibilities and lends natural dignity to the chorale, whereas a Gedackt 4' is quite unsatisfactory for this purpose. It is comparable to a soprano voice trying to furnish a bass line as the fundament for a bass voice. A Regal 8' goes out of tune very easily and does not provide the same stately sound as a Gedackt 8'.

> *A Regal now and again*
> *Causes organists some pain.*
> *Reed stops do sound on occasion*
> *Rather like a fool's creation,*
> *But when pure and of good kind,*
> *They refresh one's heart and mind.*

That is what the ancients used to say. In addition to Gedackt 8' one might specify a 4' stop, open or stopped, then Octave 2' and a Scharf. All open stops must be so congenially designed as to blend well in the ensemble. Likewise, the stopped ranks must be so related to each other that their respective scaling deos not constitute a contrast in width too large to yield dependable tuning. If one desires to exceed a basic specification of four stops, one might add a Quint 3' [i.e. 2⅔'] and possibly round it off with a Tierce. The Tierce must not be larger than 1⅗', otherwise it sounds too abrasive. It is also of no use in any small organ. For even with simple chords in full ensemble it does not sound very good, particularly without the Quint 3'. But in passage work [*i.e.* monodic textures] the Tierce adds nice variety. If an organ is to be larger yet, a stopped Subbass 16' (perhaps of wood) might next be specified. After that, any variety of stops may be added according to individual tastes. But it is not advisable to specify too many reeds. Alas, how many of them do go to ruin! One organist knows how to maintain them well, another does not. A brief comment on tonal design must yet be added: it has happened that organs [even] with two manual divisions have been built without a single 8' stop. At best, they may have had a useless Regal [8'] which could hardly provide bass functions. A pedal division with a Subbass 16' was not even considered, even though that stop is splendid for congregational singing as well as for other musical functions.

But, such indispensable stops are not the organ builders' first choice since they require more work and materials and, consequently, are most costly. Therefore the specifications are now and then drawn up by the organ builders themselves, in which case a multitude of small ranks often constitutes the stop list. Although these stops do not yield any sonority, an organ such as this is on paper quite impressive with its many stops, and one can claim: the more stops the higher the price. But the unsuspecting purchasers are shrewdly kept in the dark as to the simple fact that for the price of a single 8' stop some three 2' stops can be built, and then some. Lest village organs will sound more like bagpipes than organs, I had to mention all this for the benefit of [rural] churches. Without a doubt, good organists [from out of town] will be consulted when large organs are to be designed, if there should not be any local specialists in residence.

In order to be of further service to my good friends, I wish to elaborate a little more on tonal design by adding the following:

Eine Disposition eines grossen Orgel-Wercks.

Ober-Werck.

1. Principal. 16
2. Qvintiten. 16
3. Octava. 8
4. Spitzfloit. 8
5. Gedack weiter mensur. 8
6. Violdigambd 8
7. Qvinta 6
8. SuperOctav. 4
9. Qvinta. 3
10. Klein Octav. 2
11. Tertia. 1⅗
12. Mixtur. 6. fach. 1
13. Fagott. 16
14. Trompet. 8

} Fuß-Thon.

Rück-Positiv.

1. Principal. 8
2. Qvintiten. 8
3. Octava. 4
4. Qvinta. 3
5. Nacht-Horn offen. 4
6. Super Octav. 2
7. Tertia. 1⅗
8. Gedackte Qvinta. 3
9. Mixtur. 4. fach. 1
10. Spitzfloit. 4
11. Fagott. 8
12. Schallmey. 4

} Fuß-Thon.

Die Brust zum 3. Clavier.

1. Principal 4
2. Qvinta Thon 8
3. Gelinde Gedack enge Mensur 8
4. Klein Gedackt 4
5. Qvinta 3
6. Octav 2
7. Spitzfloit. 2
8. Qvinta Thon 4
9. Feldfloit 1
10. Tertia 1⅗
11. Mixtur 3. fach —
12. Lieblich Regal 8

} Fuß-Thon.

Baß-Lade.

1. Principal 16
2. Groß-Untersatz 32
3. Subbaß 16
4. Octava 8
5. Gedackt 8
6. Super Octava 4
7. Kleine Octava 2
8. Walt Flöit Baß 1
9. Mixtur. 4. Fach 1
10. Posaun 16
11. Trompet 8
12. Cornet 2

} Fuß-Thon.

Sum.

STOP LIST OF A LARGE ORGAN

[In modern rather than Werckmeister's archaic spelling]

Oberwerk [*i.e.* Great]
1. Principal 16'
2. Quintadena 16'
3. Octave 8'
4. Spitzflöte 8'
5. Gedackt (wide) 8'
6. Viola da gamba 8'
7. Quint 6' [*i.e.* 5⅓']
8. Superoctave 4'
9. Quinte 3' [*i.e.* 2⅔']
10. Kleinoctave 2'
11. Tierce 1⅗'
12. Mixture VI 1'
13. Fagott 16'
14. Trompete 8'

Rückpositiv
1. Principal 8'
2. Quintadena 8'
3. Octave 4'
4. Quint 3' [*i.e.* 2⅔']
5. Nachthorn (open) 4'
6. Superoctave 2'
7. Tierce 1⅗'
8. Gedackt Quint 3'
   [*i.e.* 2⅔']
9. Mixture IV 1'
10. Spitzflöte 4'
11. Fagott 8'
12. Schalmei 4'

Brustwerk (on third manual)
1. Principal 4'
2. Quintatön 8'
3. Gelind [lieblich]
   Gedackt (narrow) 8'
4. Kleingedackt 4'
5. Quinte 3' [*i.e.* 2⅔']
6. Octave 2'
7. Spitzflöte 2'
8. Quintatön 4'
9. Feldflöte 1'
10. Tierce 1⅗'
11. Mixture III — [*sic*]
12. Lieblich Regal 8'

Bass Chest [*i.e.* Pedal]
1. Principal 16'
2. Gross-Untersatz 32'
3. Subbass 16'
4. Octave 8'
5. Gedackt 8'
6. Superoctave 4'
7. Kleinoctave 2'
8. Waldflötenbass 1'
9. Mixture IV 1'
10. Posaune 16'
11. Trompete 8'
12. Cornet 2'

This totals 50 stops. Should one desire four manuals, the following stops might be placed on a separate chest behind the main [case]:
first a Gelind [lieblich] Gedackt 8', [then] Kleingedackt 4', Nasat
3', Sifflöte 2', Kleingedackt 2', Mixture III, Vox humana 8'. If these
stops can be placed in a separate box, it sounds as from a distance
and is very pleasant to listen to. But if this were to prove too com-
plicated, one might install [these stops] in lieu of the Brustwerk or
of the Rückpositiv (since the latter is not very popular these days,
anyway). An organ of this size [i.e. three manuals and pedal] might
have such auxiliary stops as two tremulants, one slow and one fast;
Zimbelstern and Pauke [i.e. tympanum; percussion].[45] This size
organ needs from five to seven bellows, each 10' long and 6' wide.
Three or four bellows would serve the manual chests and two or
three bellows the pedal chests. This [separation of pedal wind] helps
to eliminate the great unsteadiness of wind which the pedal, owing
to its large pipes, commonly causes. By way of further comment on
this specification, it should be pointed out that the Principal 16' in
the Oberwerk is not imperative. A Principal 8' might well take its
place, considering that such a large stop has little appeal in a manual
division. Obviously, in that case the Octave 8' would be eliminated
as needless duplication of the Principal 8'. Likewise, the Quint 6'
would be omitted. In the Rückpositiv a Principal 4' would replace
the Principal 8' in the event of the Oberwerk's being based on 8'
principal level. The Octave 4' of the Rückpositiv might be exchanged
for a Gedackt 8'. Some people might opt for a Principal 32' rather
than the Principal 16' in the Pedal, if the Oberwerk has a Principal
16'. I advise against this, since such large [pipe] bodies rarely allow
for good voicing, offer little pleasure to the ear and are so costly that
one single pipe nearly amounts to the price of a small organ. Such a
stop should be called Sham Braggart, for it brags by looks only, but
is a veritable sham with regard to audibility. In this case a Gedackt
16' does more in the manual than a Principal 16', [just as] a Gedackt
32' in the Pedal is better than a Principal 32', since it costs less,

---

45Adlung, *Musica*, Vol. I, p. 194, states flatly: *"Guckguck* [*i.e.* cuckoo],
Trommel [*i.e.* drum], *Pauke*, [*i.e.* tympanum] and *Vogelsang* [*i.e.* bird call]
are absurdities no longer included in modern organs; they are of no other
use than making audiences laugh. The *Stern* is still used on occasions . . . ."

speaks more promptly and is only made of wood. It is conceivable, therefore, that such a large organ might have a Gedackt 16' in the [main] manual [division] and a Quintadena 16' in the Rückpositiv, as is indeed the case in various instances. Other stops [in our sample specification] may also be altered according to individual preferences. One person insists on this, another demands that. Care must be taken, however, that the manuals are not assigned larger stops than the Pedal, [an error] I have actually encountered. It has also been known to happen that only one single Subbass was specified for the Pedal, which then could not hold its own against the full organ. Therefore, it would be better if pull-down pedals were built, either by means of separate pallets or mechanical hookup, in instruments too small to allow for a completely equipped Pedal chest. In large, elaborate organs where one can afford separation, an independent Pedal is ideal, since it allows for ample variety. In these matters one must exercise good judgment and discernment. I know [for example] of one organ, where the low octave in the pedal is permanently coupled to the Oberwerk, whereas the Subbass speaks only in the upper pedal octave. The absurdity of this arrangement is self-evident to any initiated person. Another organ builder replaced the Subbass in the Pedal with a miserable reed — after all, the manual did have a Quintadena 16': some smart exchange by way of renovation!

In a large organ the builder might avail himself of different scaling [between divisions]. For example, [relatively] wide-scaled pipework might be used in the Oberwerk and Pedal, intermediate scaling in the second manual and quite narrow scaling in the third. Each division would have to be scaled according to a unified design, otherwise a mish-mash would result. [With organ builders] this is an area of reticence. Each organ builder prefers to stick to the scales he has drawn up once and for all. But I can avow that each manual would produce its own characteristic sound and would be that much more pleasant to the ear. For one person likes the sound of wide-scaled pipes, another loves that of narrow-scaled stops, and in this manner many could be pleased. From the foregoing discussion one may derive some insights in selecting stops for small and large organ specifications. Therefore, a more detailed treatment is not here in order.

For further reading one might turn to Chapter 9 [*sic*]⁴⁶ of Michael
Praetorius' Vol. II of *Syntagma Musicum*.

  Since some people are getting entangled in heated arguments over
the legendary method of distinguishing between whole, half, and
quarter organs, I wish to address myself to this issue: one needs to
know that the ancients considered an instrument a whole organ if it
had open Principal 16′ in the manual — for a 32′ stop is of no use in
a manual. If an instrument's principal basis was 8′, they called it a
half organ; with a Principal 4′ it was called a quarter organ; with a
Principal 2′ an eighth [Werckmeister says "half-quarter"] organ,
notwithstanding the presence of lower-pitched stopped ranks. Many
people have maintained this terminology, and well they might continue with such usage. Additional information can be gleaned from
Praetorius' *Syntagma*, Vol. II, Part 3, Chapter 10⁴⁷ and Part 4,
Chapter 1. If one were to think in terms of completeness of stop
selection, one could never find a whole organ (literally speaking),
for there is such a great variety of existing and yet to be invented
stops that it would be quite impossible to place them all into one
organ. Therefore, one always selects such stops for a specification
as will be of greatest usefulness and as will satisfy one's personal preferences. But it must be remembered that constituent [stops]
of the full organ [*i.e.* plenum sound] ought not to be omitted. The
4′, 3′, 2′, 1′ stops, mixtures and the like all must be made according
to a unified [scaling] scheme, otherwise they will not hold up⁴⁸ in
the full ensemble and will not get along very well together. For
even after they have been quite accurately tuned, they will go their
own ways [*i.e.* the ranks will lose tuning by individual pipes rather
than flat or sharp as a chorus] when the weather changes, as I have
previously remarked. Much could also be written about unusual stop
nomenclature, if opportunity should offer. For often one finds the

------

⁴⁶Werckmeister probably refers to Part 5 of Vol. II, *De Organographia*,
in which Praetorius prints original specifications of famous organs along
with seven model specifications of his own design.

  ⁴⁷Praetorius records the following additional terminology: 16′ principal,
manual = *Gross Principal Werk*; 8′ principal, manual = *Aequal Principal
Werk*; 4′ principal, manual = *Octav*, or *Klein Principal Werk*.

  ⁴⁸Werckmeister most likely refers to tuning.

oddest derivations relating neither to sound nor to facts. Indeed, the etymology of some stop names is quite obscure, but what has been *usu receptum* [sanctioned by usage] might as well be retained. On some organs one finds stop designations in totally alien terms, so that no uninitiated person can exercise his whim on the instrument during the absence of the appointed organist. For the benefit of those who wish to know these terms, I am listing the most important:

Regula primaria	Principal
Quintitenens	Quintatön
Coni	Spitzflöte, Spielflöte
Tibia Sylvestris	Waldflöte
Tibia Angusta	Dulzflöte
Diapason	Octave
Diapente	Quint
Disdiapason	Superoctave
Diapente pileata	Nasat
Miscella acuta	Mixture
Pileata major	Grossgedackt
Pileata minor	Kleingedackt
Tibia Vulgaris	Blockflöte
Ditonus sive Tertia	Tierce 1⅗'
Piffaro	Schalmei
Pileata maxima	Untersatz, Subbass
Fistula rurestris	Feldflöte, Bauernflöte
Buccina	Posaune
Tuba	Trompete
Fagotto	Dulzian
Cornu	Cornet
Epistomium	[Sperr-] Ventil

Chapter Twenty-Two.

OFTEN such large pipes as low G sharp and F sharp are omit-ted[49] which, in a present-day organ, constitutes a major defect. Also, those short octaves in the bass range which retain G sharp and F sharp[50] are anything but praiseworthy, since they require [still] more abnormal fingering than the other [short] octaves. Conse-quently, if an organist wants to become as fluent in this octave as in the normal octaves [of the keyboard] he will have to practice hard in order to become two organists in one, in a manner of speaking. For what applies to the normal octave becomes here quite the opposite in many ways. For example, take the progression E [lower of second double-key] to F sharp [upper of first double-key] to D [lower of first double-key] to G [third lower key] to E [lower of second double-key] to G sharp [upper of second double-key] to A [fourth lower key]. In this sequence E to F sharp is contrary [to normal mo-tion], F sharp to D is rather unusual. The same is true of D-G, G-E, again contrary [to usage] and so forth. Thus the normal order of the keyboard is totally contradicted and a great deal of special effort in practicing is required. It is ridiculous to resort to prolixity, detours and bombast in order to achieve something that could be attained by a more direct and more comfortable route. I, for one, have yet to see an organist who is as adept in the low [*i.e.* short] octave as he is in the other octaves. So far I have heard no other defense [of the short octave] than that it allows reaching [with one hand] an octave

---

49Werckmeister seems to refer to the short octave in which the pipes (but not their corresponding keys) F sharp and G sharp were omitted along with the lowest four pipes *and* keys. Thus, the short octave consisted of five white and three black keys to which the pipes were often allotted as follows: Upper keys: D E Bb; Lower keys: C F G A B.

50Presumably, in such a short octave, the first two of the three black keys would be double-keys yielding the following scheme of pitch allotment:

secondary upper keys			F#	G#		
upper keys			D	E	Bb	
lower keys	C	F	G	A	B	

and a third [*i.e.* a tenth]. That is a rather poor expedient. For it could hardly be considered advantageous to spoil a keyboard, particularly in the bass range, just because one can reach with one hand the two thirds [in the chords] D-d-f sharp and E-e-g sharp. Not only is the low range unsuitable to [such] thirds, but we also have a right hand with which we can accommodate [chord spacing] in many more ways than these thirds could ever effect. To sum up, it is a *praeconcepta opinio* [preconceived notion] and an unfortunate convention to which many still adhere who do not know any better. Many also display this frailty [of judgment]: because their teachers espoused it, it cannot be otherwise. If he held this irrational opinion, the disciple surely must not ditch it.

Chapter Twenty-Three.

IT is also necessary to spell out as much as possible every detail in the contract: how, where and which things should be done; the composition of metal alloys; board and room arrangements [for installation crew].[51] Otherwise one is likely to run into unforeseen snags. One has to ensure organ placement not too close to [outside] walls and away from exposure to [outside] air and [direct] sunlight. In order to prevent any oversights, it is absolutely necessary that a good organist, experienced in such matters, be commissioned to supervise carefully the building of the organ and to offer advice on how to do things in the most practical and the most durable manner. Such consultations and gentle reminders ought not to be resented by an organ builder, since a well versed organist has plenty of experience concerning adverse effects on the organ by climatic conditions. He will anticipate troubles and identify weak construction features which the organ builder might never have considered and which at

---

[51]Contrary to present-day procedures, most organ builders up to the late eighteenth century built their instruments on site, *i.e.* in the town where the instrument was to be placed.

the occasion of the final proofing — when the organ is completely installed and encased — might not easily be seen and detected. But even if they were to be found then, they would hardly be corrected. Usually, at that stage, the damage has to be borne by the church, although it could have been prevented by diligent supervision and consultation. Unfortunately, the arrogance and envy of many an organ builder are so great that he will not tolerate any organist around his work. On the other hand, an organist ought not to impose unreasonable demands on the organ builder, lest he be chastised by a genuine organ builder for being a smart aleck.

Chapter Twenty-Four.

IT is also absolutely necessary and advantageous to retain a knowledgeable organist for the planning of and contracting for an organ renovation. He should decide on what actually needs to be renovated. For if an unconscionable organ builder happens to be commissioned, he will tear up the good along with the bad, all in one heap (like the [big bad] wolf) so as to create the bigger a job for himself. Many a builder has dismantled something far better than what he built in its stead. Many a builder hauls away a better wind chest than the new chest he has built, and many such old chests have been profitably resold for new. The same is true of [old] bellows for which merely new folds were made. These and similar [fraudulent practices] are quite common. Frequently in the course of such renovations large ranks are replaced by little hissers. Then, at another location, these [large] pipes come in handy for the organ builder. In these matters, an organist must not let himself be duped. Rather, he should explain with well reasoned arguments to the elders, how this or that might be saved and repaired.

A certain organ builder once had to renovate an organ. When he had completed his work, but had not yet secured another job, he suddenly claimed that the old wind chest was no longer serviceable, even though he had found nothing wrong with it at the outset. In order to paste the appearance of credulity onto [the thin surface of] his pretence and intrigues, he proceeded to block the wind in the wind trunk so that just enough wind could get through to supply two or three stops. These would sound good enough, but the full organ, particularly in full textures, sounded out of tune because of the reduced inflow. Two or three keys alone, however, sounded in tune even with full organ, but everything went out of tune in full textures. The organ builder duly blamed the wind chest, even though [such a condition] could not possibly be caused by wind leakage [in the chest]. Neither could the defect be ascribed to insufficient size of pallets, otherwise a single key also should have sounded dull and out of tune, and wind leakage at the top boards and sliders would have had to affect one or two keys [as much as full chords]. Thus, it became quite clear that the wind in the trunk had been [intentionally] blocked, otherwise the organ builder might have enjoyed a prolonged stay and continued employment in addition to perhaps acquiring a better wind chest than that which he proposed to build. Snow jobs such as this are widespread, I cannot relate them without agitation. Once again, I shall have earned little gratitude from some builders [with the preceding account]. I do always exclude honest people, but the dishonest might as yet be accused by their own consciences, should these ever be aroused. May God grant that they have a change of heart and reform while there is still time.

Once an organ has been inspected by the expert (the local organist might also be consulted, since he is familiar with the circumstances), it is best to compile a detailed and concisely spelled out list of all defects and items with a view to implementation of the planned renovation. Generalizations in a contract [for renovation] should rightly be challenged by the organ builder. For example, the organ [to be renovated] may suffer from a congenital defect, too-small key channels. Such a defect he could correct only by installing new wind chests. Any planned alteration of the instrument's original specification should also be included in the contract. Smaller defects that cannot possibly be specified in advance must be corrected without hedging by the builder. If new bellows are to be installed, the wind pressure of the old bellows, as measured by the wind gauge, must be adequately replicated, otherwise the entire pipe work would have to be revoiced and tuned.

Chapter Twenty-Five.

IT had been my original intention to provide a table of approximate quantities and kinds of materials needed for building large or small organs. To that end, I had compiled data on the relative weight of individual pipes as well as entire ranks and on the composition of alloys, utilizing several notebooks and construction ledgers which were acquired posthumously from prominent organ builders of the past and present. But since times are changing; since purchasing costs and local economic conditions vary greatly; and because some organ builders might even lodge complaints over my public disclosure of their business secrets, I have decided to bypass these subject matters and, for the present time, to forego further discussion.[52] A conscientious organ builder will, of his own accord, beware of overcharging the church, realizing how grave a sin it is to acquire church goods by unjust means. Nevertheless, it is quite in order to solicit information concerning the specifications and cost of organs in the vicinity, concerning honesty of transactions [on the part of the builder] and any other pertinent aspects. This can then provide some basis for [further] considerations. In this context I must add the following remark: once a genuine organ builder has been selected and retained, one must not be too stingy in the negotiations. For if an organ builder is supposed to earn his bread and provide for his wife and children by his profession, he must not be dealt with so miserly. Out of curiosity and to find out for myself just what it takes, I have had some organs built in my house at my own expense. I can truthfully state that if an organ builder could not profit any more than I did in this venture, his wife and children should have to go begging. Since I had thought

---

[52]However, in Chapter 26 this subject matter is treated in considerable detail.

of it merely as a *Parergon* [hobby], I have now decided to discontinue [building organs, whereas professional organ builders do not have this option].

An organ builder should occasionally develop new ideas of his own, should constantly evolve new approaches and test out his inventions so that this most laudable art be perpetuated, exalted and advanced to the praise of God. It is common knowledge that this profession involves not only the mechanical aptitudes of artisans and craftsmen but derives its principles also from mathematics, arithmetic and physics. In short, who could enumerate all contingencies to be expected from these [multifaceted prerequisites]! If such a man is incapable of *Rationes* [the ability of systematic thinking] and has not already profited from experience, how can the churches be assured that [his] work is reliable, durable and efficient? For it is impossible, even for a fellow with a brilliant head [on his shoulders], to learn everything there is to know during his years of training, even if he is a journeyman for twenty years. Therefore, it is just as impossible to commit to writing everything that could conceivably occur at an organ proofing. At times not one out of a hundred can find the cause of an unpleasant sound. Of course, if one fails to find the real cause, one can always resort to blaming the wolf. But there might never have been a need to plead wolves' howling if many a fellow had paid attention from the outset to well proportioned [scaling of] the pipe work, to neat joinery in his windchest construction and to good [drawing board] design. Designing an organ is time-consuming and must be recognized as [part of the overall project] deserving remuneration. Even though designing does not involve [manual] work [at the building site], such mental deliberations are just as important. On the other hand, I do not wish to open the door to laziness disguised as organ designing.

Since I have mentioned the wind gauge [see footnote 42] several times (incidentally, it also is a factor in designing), and since many do not know what kind of instrument it is, I shall briefly describe it:

First one fashions a little metal box, approximately two or three inches long and half as wide and deep. Then, one inserts through its lid a wind tube, approximately one half inch in diameter and bent in such a manner that one can plug it in [*e.g.* into a wind-trunk].

Close to this tube, one fastens [in the same manner] another short little duct, inserting into it a glass tube also approximately one half inch in diameter. Next, a little measure, six inches or one-fourth yard [*Elle*] long and calibrated into 60 degrees, is placed [upright] next to the glass tube. If wind is admitted, one can see how high it pushes [the water][53] and whether [the wind pressure] is even or shaking. This calibration into 60 degrees is used by various eminent builders. It would be desirable that this norm be adopted uniformly by [all] organ builders. Then one could examine [by a uniform standard] all organs with respect to strong or weak, even or uneven wind pressure. Having examined many organs, I have found considerable wind pressure variations [from one to another]: 15°, 20°, 30°, up to 40°, even 45°. A wind pressure of 15° to 20° is miserable. Such an organ is bound to speak sleepily and lazily. A pressure of 30° is barely acceptable; the most comfortable range is between 35° and 40°. In some of the fine old organs, I have frequently measured 35° to 36° of pressure.[54] This wind pressure works admirably if there is enough inflow to the large labial and lingual ranks. I have often found that [adequate] inflow can [favorably] affect the large ranks. For example, whereas the low Subbass pipes in organs with wind pressure as weak as 32° did little more than panting, they gained a strong and clear sound and boomed along nicely when the wind inflow was increased. Concerning the manufacture of a wind gauge, there are still some additional considerations which, for the sake of brevity, I cannot here mention. An amateur curious enough will surely do his own research. This little instrument leads to all manner of speculation. For example, a four year old child can blow the *liquorem* [the fluid, *i.e.* the water] entirely out of [the open end of] the glass tube, yet ten or more bellows with a [combined] weighting amounting to many hundredweights cannot drive the water that high. Again, one man, blowing into a bellows through a narrow

---

[53]Werckmeister fails to mention here that the "little metal box" contains water. A further minor error results from measuring only the height of the water in the tube. As the water rises in the tube the level falls in the box. The *difference* between the two levels is the critical measurement.

[54]This pressure (35°-36°) which Werckmeister seems to consider ideal, converts to ca. 80 mm, or 3¼".

tube, can raise several hundredweights, provided the bellows is well sealed with glue so that the small quantity of wind is not lost in the cracks and wood pores. This is an amusing sight to behold. This phenomenon suggests [an analogy with] the cause of an earthquake. An intelligent person will easily understand the causal similarities.

Chapter Twenty-Six.

IN order to satisfy somewhat [the expectations of] several of my friends, I shall, after all, supply the [average] weight of some of the more common ranks, relying on the posthumously acquired logs of various organ builders. In an effort to further verify these data, I have purchased the entire pipe work of an old organ, amounting to a total weight of five hundredweights, and thereby I have confirmed [the following data]:[55]

Principal 8', tin; from C, D, E, F, F sharp, G, G sharp up to c″ [c‴?]:	165 lb.; others may have 200 lb.; still others 220 lb.
Principal 4':	60 lb.; some 85 lb.
Gedackt 8', fairly good metal:	127 lb.; others 140 lb.; others 120 lb.
Quintade 16':	260 lb.; others 271 lb.
Quintatön 8':	116 lb.; others 125 lb.
Octave 4':	49 lb.; others 54 lb.
Quint 3':	22 lb.; others 25 lb.
Superoctave 2':	15 lb.; others 18 lb.
Gedackt 4':	72 lb.; alii [others] 76 lb.

[55]In the absence of exact information concerning Werckmeister's weight scale, 1 pound might be assumed to have measured between 450 g. and 500 g. (The pound was subdivided into 30 or 32 Lot; 1 Lot approximates ½ ounce).

Mixture V:	60 lb.; the largest pipe is 1′ long.
Mixture IV:	can weigh as much as 90 lb. if the largest pipe is of 2′ length.
Superoctave 1′:	10 lb.
Mixture III, 1′:	32 lb.

It must be remembered that a certain differential factor is inevitable: one [builder] applies wider scaling than another; one uses slightly stronger metal for the pipe work than another; one may use longer pipe feet; another may use more lead than others. Obviously, the pipes need to be sturdy. This alone accounts for certain variances. Not even the same builder can exactly duplicate [pipe weights]. Nevertheless, a little information enabling the purchaser to handle his transaction so as not to be overcharged comes in handy. These average weights, incidentally, tally with the specifications of the famous organ builder, Arp Schnitger, who has built from scratch the large organ in the Johanniskirche of Magdeburg.[56] This instrument is being applauded by many knowledgeable people, particularly for its reed stops, and I must confess to having been much delighted with it upon a painstaking visual and aural examination. Some organ builders are very cunning in bamboozling church officials as to how they upgrade common metal by adding more than half tin. Upon close examination their metal hardly contains one-eighth tin. They also fraudulently claim to use only pure tin for principals, whereas in reality they barely add one third. It is common knowledge that pure tin is often so brittle and hard that one cannot very well use it. No honest organ builder will hold it against me that I have made these disclosures. These are not hearsay, rather they are based on personal experiences which have served to acquaint me with such habitual practices of unscrupulous organ builders. I call upon honest builders as my witnesses. Poor metal containing much lead cannot withstand corrosion [see footnote 9], and the large pipes usually settle or even bend to the floor. Of course, if a congregation accepts such poor metal, the organ builder is [home] free. I have seen a specification in which the organ builder has charged the congregation for twice the normal weight of the stops. Among others, a

---

[56]Built in 1689-95, this instrument had three manual divisions and 62 stops.

Bauernflöte was itemized as weighing ½ hundredweight, whereas its average weight does not exceed 10 lb. This is the kind of conspicuous fraud that hurts many a decent builder who is not at all blameworthy. In the same manner, all the other stops had been itemized, their claimed weights exceeding by more than double the average weight.

In spite of considerable variance in alloys and metal mixtures, reflecting personal preferences [of the builder] or [contractual] specifications [by the purchaser], I have decided to list some of the more common [ratios]. A good admixture is one third tin, namely 2 lb. lead and 1 lb. tin. This ratio yields good metal which can be used for [pipes] in[side] the organ. One might even use it for a second-rate principal, especially in rural churches. If one desires a higher grade metal for principals, one might choose an alloy of half lead and half tin. If they [the principals] are to be better yet, one uses two parts tin and one part lead. Pure tin is rarely used, since it is hard to work with. If one wishes to use lower [tin content] metal, he might use 3 lb. lead and 1 lb. tin, that is, one fourth tin. Some even use one sixth, seventh, eighth, ninth, and one tenth tin, but less than that is hardly feasible. Such inferior metals might be so upgraded through the regulus[57] as to appear as white and hard as tin. However, not everyone succeeds in extracting the regulus from the antimony.[58] Since, moreover, it is also a health hazard,[59] I do not advise it. Some people have experimented with refining [techniques] using marcasite,[60] but it does not work.

It serves no purpose to list individual pipe weights, otherwise I should gladly do so. But another point to be carefully observed and watched in organ proofings is the matter of collusion between ex-

---

[57]*Regulus,* metalloid element in the lead. Werckmeister's unclear wording may describe a refining process: "Thus with the aid of antimony the [presumably undesirable] regulus is smelted out to achieve an [appearance of] higher-grade metal."

[58]Metalloid element often alloyed with lead in order to harden it.

[59]Although antimony was considered a health hazard, lead was the real culprit.

[60]Coloquially known as "white iron," this is a mineral, iron disulfide.

aminers and organ builder: in return for a [stringed keyboard] instrument or a clavichord, one might certify an organ to be flawless
in every respect, even if it were afflicted with a thousand defects. Unfortunately, this happens quite often. The alert Praetorius deplores,
[*op. cit.*] Vol. II, p. 109, how in his time unconscionable people
conspired to fleece the church for shameful profits. I am, obviously,
not referring to the honorarium or gratuity to which an organist is
traditionally and quite rightly entitled upon completion of his
visitation and trial of an organ. A conscientious examiner may by
rights accept [an honorarium], the more so as he may have spoiled
his clothing by crawling around inside the organ, and as he may have
had to swallow not only dirt and dust but also ill humoured remarks
and secret distress. He may even have incurred the overt enmity of
the organ builder for the sake of good old truth. No, I do not refer
to such legitimate gratuities. What I do have in mind is the hypocrisy
that now and then unites organist and organ builder.

Chapter Twenty-Seven.

IT even happens quite regularly that consultants and church elders,
having recommended such an [incapable] organ builder, seek to
cover up and defend the latter's fraud or shoddy work, no matter
how [ill] the church might have been served. The reason is rather
obvious: first, they are embarrassed by their failure to have chosen
better people and by thus being responsible for the loss incurred by
the church and congregation. Secondly, they may even have received
a kickback from the organ builder. A conscientious examiner will
quickly accept [an invitation]; note in writing all defects; and for-
ward [his report] to the church officials. They [in turn] will con-
front the builder in the presence of the examiners. If the organ builder can reasonably explain the [cited] irregularities, one might ac-
quiesce. For it is common knowledge that not one organ in all the
world is without its deficiencies. But I am referring to major defects,

such as: wind runs in the pallets, at the sliders or anywhere in the channels, resulting in quite audible hissing or murmuring within one [or the other] stop; shaking, trembling or gulping which so impairs steadiness [of organ sound] that one perceives continuous quivering; unsteady or insufficient wind requiring no less drastic corrective measures than overhauling the wind chests (if wind loss caused by Swedish stabs [*i.e.* bleed holes] or by other apertures is excessive) or additions to or complete rebuilding of the bellows; in short anything that, in effect, spoils the harmony of an organ and that cannot be corrected without major expense must be considered a major defect. Either an organ builder agrees to making alterations and corrections at no cost [to the church], or he must relinquish as much money [from his total take] as will pay for the repair work by another [builder]. However, such gross defects occur very infrequently. One would have to be an awful quack of an organ builder to have bungled so badly as to be forcibly replaced by another builder. Yet, since there are such precedents, it was necessary to mention them, so that [the general public] might beware of bunglers.

Chapter Twenty-Eight.

IF the church officials are content to accept such inferior work, the examiners, having noted [the defects], are under no further obligations. There may be some minor defects which the organ builder might not have corrected just yet [*i.e.* at the time of the official proofing]. For example, one or the other pipe might have been cut up a little too high and sound sore, a little duller than, and not quite matching with, the other pipes; or a little worm hole just below a slider causes wind seepage, occasionally accompanied by a rustling noise; or one can hear a harmless little run in the chest. These and similar flaws one might let pass. However, this should not be invoked by some careless *Socius* [journeyman; fellow] as though it were of no consequence. No, it is mentioned here only to prevent making a mountain out of a molehill and to avoid premature criticism of an honest organ builder who otherwise has expended greatest diligence. Well balanced and regulated voicing is very important. Therefore, an examiner must note all [voicing] flaws. Whatever can be corrected among these must be attended to immediately; whatever cannot be corrected will have to remain as it is. But the major defects must be separately listed and brought to the attention of the church officials, also with a view to what they might spell for the future. Minor defects might be explained [to the officials] as inconsequential lest they suspect the organ builder [needlessly] and so that they can accept [the instrument in good conscience]. At the same time they should make him promise to live up to the usual warranty provisions and to correct serious defects that might develop during that period. However, any damage caused by carelessness or vandalism during the warranty year is not the organ builder's responsibility. He must be paid for repairing such damage. Usually, however, when an organ builder has done diligent, good and dependable work, he will be presented with a bonus, his journeymen and apprentices will receive gratuities, and the organ proofing will conclude with a dinner complete with toasts of recognition and wide-ranging and good conversation.

Chapter Twenty-Nine.

I HAVE also been requested to present a special description of how to draw and change the voices of an organ [i.e. how to approach registration]. But I consider such a discussion superfluous, assuming that everybody endowed with a normal sense of hearing can easily perceive how well one [stop] goes with another. For the benefit of the uninitiated and of beginners, however, I might unambiguously state that one does not like to draw together two stops of identical pitch[61] that are dissimilarly scaled. For no matter how accurately they may be tuned, their proportions, as far as the wide-scaled pipes are concerned, do not go together very well. One can clearly discern two separate entities, usually underscored by uneven wind.[62] Indeed, wide scales diverge so much from narrow scales under the influence of changes in weather, that one can hardly use them [*i.e.* wide-scaled and narrow-scaled ranks] together, even on pitch levels an octave apart. For in a dense atmosphere [see footnote 36], the wide-scaled [ranks] experience a lack of incisiveness and show discrepancies [even] among themselves. Similarly, nobody could have such a strange sense of hearing as to draw, for example, a Quint 3' as fundamental stop to which he adds other higher-pitched voices; or to draw a Quint with just one gentle Gedackt for playing full, slow chords; that would sound strange! A practiced organist can exchange [and use] against each other virtually all the stops. [The main considera- tion is that] they all must be used according to the [musical] re- quirements; the large ranks in slow, majestic chordal textures; [com- binations with] Quint and Tierce, also called Sesquialtera, for fast passages, *coloribus* [coloraturas in the manner of the colorists] and figures. A good ear is the best criterion. Therefore, the beginner should occasionally[63] go to the church alone, in order to critically listen to his manner of registration and to learn to comprehend the

---

[61]Werckmeister's term *Aequalstimmen* refers to a combination of one wide-scaled and one narrow-scaled labial rank, either of 8' pitch, (*aequal*, according to Praetorius, means equal to the pitch level of the human voice, *i.e.* 8'), or (by the definitions of such later writers as Adlung and Mattheson) of any identical pitch level. His primary concern seems to be the resulting heterogeneous tone color. But he does also seem to imply that an ill chosen registration uses more than its fair share of wind. One or two generations later, Dom Bédos warns his French colleagues not to use wind-wasting reg- istrations (usually involving tremulants in chordal textures).

[62]Literally, this sentence reads: "One also perceives the difference of equality as predominant feature; thereto, then, uneven wind can aid greatly."

[63]Much practicing and teaching was done in the home on smaller instru- ments, positiv, clavichord and harpsichord. Using the large instrument in the church for practice purposes involved having to hire the Calcants (bellows treaders) on "overtime" basis.

nature of each stop. For one thing is certain: not every registrational approach works with all stops. Therefore, discerning musical judgment and a good ear are the best means.

Chapter Thirty.

HERE I cannot resist elaborating on what is called the Sesquialtera.[64] As is well known, the ratio of the Sesquialtera yields [the interval of the] fifth. That is why the ancients placed a Quint, commonly called 3′, as I have derived from a letter by Mich. Praetorius to one of his good friends. Often they added in the specifications for each key [of such a stop] a second, smaller pipe which, in relation to the first, sounded a [major] sixth. In relation to the fundamental pitch of its key it sounded *Tertiam Primo-Compositam* [a predetermined, fixed (major) third]. For example, in relation to C of Principal 4′, the ancient so-called Sesquialtera sounds G-e; on the [4′ fundamental] key D, this Sesquialtera sounds A-f sharp and so on throughout the entire keyboard without alterations [*i.e.* breaks]. Therefore, the stop Sesquialtera which the same Praetorius first discovered in 1620 in the Cathedral Church of Hildesheim, was quite accurrately so named. For *a Potiori fit denominatio* [the name reflects the most prominent (feature)]: the pipe sounding the fifth of the fundamental is larger[*i.e.* more prominent] than its higher-pitched companion which sounds *Tertiam primo compositam* [the predetermined (major) third] of the fundamental key and is not so prominent in size. Later, when building Sesquialteras was modified by omitting the larger pipe which sounds the fifth — because all organs

---

[64]The prefix *sesqui-* (half again as much) together with *altera* (two) alludes to the ratio 3:2; 3 contains 2 and one half again as much, namely 1. Sesquialtera then, is: 2/2 + ½ = 3/2, *i.e.* the interval of the fifth. As will be seen, Werckmeister applies this prefix to other numbers as well, *e.g.* sesquiquarta: 4/4 + ¼ = 5/4, *i.e.* the interval of the third.

have [such fifths] anyway as [separate] Quint stops — the name Sesquialtera remained.

Since this was a misnomer, inasmuch as a Quint rather than a Tierce deserves this designation, much disputing and much confusion have been caused by it. Therefore, I have briefly explained why the currently called Sesquialtera [stop] with just one pipe per key, can by rights only be called a Tierce according to its nature. He who prefers an alien term may call it *Ditonus* [*sive Tertia*]; or, with reference to its interval ratio, *Sesquiquarta*, [*i.e.*] $5/4$; or *dupla* [twice as big] *Sesquiquarta*, [*i.e.*] $5/2$; or, relating it to 8′ basis, *Quintupla* [fivefold], in figures [representing the string length of the monochord]: $1/5$; and so forth; *decupla* [tenfold], relating to 16′ basis, in figures: 1/10. But, returning to the Quint: by strict mathematical standards it cannot be designated as a 3′ [stop]. For if C is 4′ long, G is only $2\frac{2}{3}$′, whereas F is [really] 3′ long. But since this [designation] has wormed its way into common usage — leave it to the organ builders — let us desist from becoming anabaptists,[65] for *verba valent sicut nummi* [words have the value of currency], and often a counterfeit penny passes more easily than a genuine coin. The Tierce in the 2′ octave is $1\frac{3}{5}$′. If it were larger by an octave [*i.e.* $3\frac{1}{5}$′], it would sound too harsh. Another stop organ builders use, commonly called Tertian, also occurs in the 2′ octave range, sounding with its larger pipe a major third and with its smaller pipe a fifth [of the fundamental key]. It is similar to the ancient Sesquialtera, except that the fifth, not the third, is the higher interval. Thus, on the [key] of 2′ c, the Tertian sounds e-g.

This [stop] is quite useful, but it would be even better if each [of its two] ranks was available as a separate stop throughout the keyboard. In this way, one would have greater flexibility. Otherwise, one might as well combine many ranks in one single stop in the manner of the very earliest builders.[66] But what would then happen to flexibility and variability in registration? Finally, it should be noted that a [single] Tierce $1\frac{3}{5}$′ together with an 8′ or 4′ stop does

---

[65]"Anabaptism," here in the sense of re-christening, *i.e.* changing the name. Werckmeister's facetious use of the term also connotes his mock horror of being charged with heresy by the building trade.

[66]Werckmeister refers to the *Blockwerk*.

not sound too good, unless a Quint 3' is available along with it. The reason is this: nature has never been fond of a vacuum, which, in fact, results from omitting the *Ternarius* [3', *i.e.* 2⅔' stop] which by its ratio 3:2 accounts for the fifths. Therefore, it is better, and really ought to be so, to draw a specification in the [interval] order 1. 2. 3. 4. 5.[67]

Chapter Thirty-One.

AFTER this [presumably, after an organ has been officially proofed and accepted], it might not at all be a bad idea to negotiate an annual service and maintenance contract with a dependable organ builder, once the usual warranty has expired. [This is particularly important] for large organs so that such instruments will always be in good condition. For not every organist knows how to take care of a defect, even though he may be adept in his own field. But assuming he knew how to do minor repair work, he still would not have at hand the proper tools and materials. Or, if an organist is too determined, he might in his zeal do more damage than good. Moreover, there is quite a difference between tuning strings[68] and pipes. If, therefore, an organist is ignorant of pipe tuning or, as the case may be, of adjusting the voicing, he ought not, under any circumstance, to remove a single pipe; for when a pipe is removed, it can very easily be put back differently and go out of tune.

In a well ordered household one can often find a medicine cabinet. When this or that [member of the family] is indisposed, one uses a home remedy. In the same manner, an organist may become the physician attending to minor problems of the organ entrusted to his

---

[67] This "order" is, in effect, the overtone series, which was to be confirmed by Sauveur in 1701.

[68] Keyboard players of the day were accustomed to tuning their own clavichords or harpsichords, but not necessarily church organs.

care. For more serious defects, however, an organ builder ought to be called. If he is dependable, particularly when under a maintenance contract, a church actually increases its capital, as the interest accruing [from such arrangements] is worth several times over the fee paid to the contracted organ builder.

Chapter Thirty-Two.

IT is certainly not to be condoned that many organists, out of vanity or fear or laziness refuse to move so much as one adjustment screw at the keyboard after a weather change; or to hook back into place a loose tracker; or to merely remove a speck of dust or dirt that may have gotten into this or the other reed pipe, particularly as it is impossible in most places to have an organ builder available on call. Therefore, it would be a good thing if an organist, in the absence of a builder, could repair minor defects, a qualification which many reasonable people consider mandatory for an organist. Concerning other qualifications of an organist, it would indeed be worth the effort to write a separate little treatise. However, *veritas odium parit* [truth produces hatred],

> *One's task each faithfully prepare,*
> *then all shall be in good repair.*[69]

Of late, church officials are increasingly being bamboozled [by applicants] when hiring an organist. For many organists are in the habit of memorizing a few tablature pieces, or they put the tablature in front of them [on the music rack].[70] Having previously practiced

---

[69]*Ein jeder lerne sein Lektion, so wird es wohl im Hause stohn*, from M. Luther's *Kleiner Katechismus*.

[70]Tablatures, *i.e.* notated music, were compiled for use at such secular occasions as dances, wedding feasts, etc.; in rural churches; in the home; and by amateurs. While professional organists were not legally or ethically prohibited from using their own or otherwise available notated music, they were expected to be able to improvise, particularly in job auditions.

these pieces, they play up a storm, and a person without technical
insight must think that they are obviously good organists, since they
[are able to] extemporize such learned music. On closer examination,
however, it becomes clear that they have used up [Werckmeister says
literally, "that they have dumped"] the full extent of their art.
Usually, they stick to the same old lyre [*Leyre*, colloquial for lute;
it has the meaning of "the same old record"] and a few memorized
tablature pieces for the rest of their lives. Every Sunday and Feast
Day they will spring them again on their listeners, whose ears must
ache in the end. Therefore, when an organist is being auditioned, he
must be given a theme to be developed in various manners. Or one
might select a few chorales and have him play variations on them
and let him transpose them. One must also examine him in thoroughbass, particularly with regard to accurate realization of the figuring.
For it is certainly not enough merely to play notes without rhythmic
stumbling. The figuring, too, must be realized with good voice leading, lest the entire texture be ruined. Those who maintain that the
figures over the bass line are not needed and that one could do without are in error. However, I have neither the space nor the time
here to refute this erroneous claim.

Some [auditors] select a beer song, thinking that an organist who
can play a Bourrée or a French chanson holds great promise for future exploits. But this is of minute significance; it takes far more [to
be a good organist].

Therefore, it should be [considered] imperative to have a good
organist play a good organ. One ought to be a little more discerning
in selecting him and should not fall for every show-off. For there
are many who are convinced they know everything and by their
gossip many a fine musician has been dragged into the gutter. They
love talking about things of which they have not got the slightest
notion, just like bagpipers or vagrant lutenists, who speak of horse
fifths, lamb thirds and cattle octaves[71] never knowing what they are
supposed to be. Some do indeed know that consecutive octaves and
fifths are forbidden, but avoiding them is quite another matter. But

---

71These nonsense words, connoting untutored crudeness, are possibly of
Werckmeister's own invention.

if ever they advance to the point where they can detect such *Vitia* [faulty progressions] it is impossible to get along with them any more. But this ought not to be so. There is more to composing good music than avoiding parallel octaves and fifths. These common *Vitia* [faults] are children's stuff, which a practiced musician avoids subconsciously.[72] His concern revolves about more substantial issues. All this I have offered with the sincerest of intentions so that one or the other applies himself to his profession with even greater dedication, seeking to learn the more thoroughly whatever he has not yet mastered to date. With regard to the matter of temperament, there is no need to add anything in particular, since the kind reader can find a detailed discussion and demonstration in our treatise on temperament[73] with an appendix on the monochord.

There are a few persons of ill will who perhaps cannot or, out of hatred, will not understand our demonstrated opinion. They state that they wish to retain the old, Praetorian [mean-tone] temperament and have accordingly proceeded to [publicly] express their doubts.[74] I have nothing against this, for who am I to legislate in this matter? But they might at least concede that the music of the time of Praetorius — by now nearly one hundred years old — was subject to differnet conditions than nowadays, when one encounters so many *fictas Transpositiones* [transpositions involving nondiatonic notes].[75] That is why the most illustrious Praetorius found a way to cope satisfactorily with the then current temperament, as is amply demonstrated in his compositions: whenever necessary, he could avail himself of a *subsemitonium*[76] on the key D sharp, and all was well.

---

[72]Literally, "for which a practiced musician does not constantly have to be on the lookout."

[73]*Musicalische Temperatur*, Frankfurt am Main and Leipzig: 1686-87, 1691.

[74]Werckmeister's term *scoptisiren* is probably a misprint of *sceptisiren* ("skepticize").

[75]Although he uses conservative terminology, Werckmeister seems to have in mind the modern ideal of transposing a mode or tonality to the greatest possible number of *affinales* or tonics.

[76]Here to be understood as "broken" or enharmonic key, *i.e.* double key; see also the discussion of the short octave in Chapter 22.

Nowadays however, when one has to make use of the entire keyboard as though in a circle [of fifths], it is quite impossible to make
do with such a keyboard [*i.e.* a keyboard of Praetorian temperament].
Since music, by the grace of God, has risen to such heights and
changed so much, it would, indeed, be incongruous not to think
of ways to improve keyboard instruments also; if for no other
reason than to avoid ruining contemporary pieces, some of which
are well composed, and making a mess of them.[77] But those who
wish to retain the old temperament find themselves reduced to
avoiding most, albeit delightful, *Transpositiones fictas* [transpositions
of modes or keys]. This is very thoughtless and tantamount to de-
spising the best contemporary composers and musicians. Therefore it
is most urgent, especially for organ builders, to develop a good and
workable temperament. For no matter how splendid and precious an
organ might be [otherwise], one could derive little pleasure and delight from it if it were not well tempered, or if it were patched up
with and spoiled by many *Subsemitonien* [*i.e.* double keys]. A person
unacquainted with any but the common [*i.e.* mean tone] temperament might try tuning D sharp just a little flat so that the fifth,
G sharp-D sharp, and the third, F sharp-D sharp, etc. do not sound
so horrible. With that, D sharp-G will still sound tolerable. Really,
our temperaments are not that much different from the ancients', as
some would have it.

Zarlinus[78] thought a good temperament could be derived from
tuning all fifths impure by two-sevenths of the comma. But this cannot be done. Even when all fifths are tuned impure by one-seventh
of the comma, the last fifth, F-c — if one starts on C [with laying
such a temperament] — differs by being four-sevenths [of the
comma] too large, something rather hard to take with one's ear. The
third, c-e, is too large by three-sevenths [of the comma]. Likewise,
C sharp-f by three-sevenths; D-f by three-sevenths; D sharp-G by
eight-sevenths; E-G sharp by three-sevenths; F-A by eight-sevenths;
F sharp-b flat by three-sevenths; G-B by three-sevenths; G sharp-c

[77]Literally, "lest a howling would arise from them," perhaps alluding to
a "tuning wolf."

[78]Latinization of Zarlino; likewise, in the following paragraph, Zerlinius
is the Latinization of an alternate spelling, Zerlini.

by eight-sevenths; A-c sharp by three-sevenths; B-D sharp by three-sevenths. While the major thirds might get away with a three-sevenths deviation, it is certainly not feasible to have the thirds, D sharp-G, F-A, G sharp-c beat by eight-sevenths [of the comma]. Especially [the intervals] f-A and D sharp-G are difficult to adjust so as to be tempered equal within all consonant contexts, nor is that advisable. For whereas the [relatively well tempered] thirds are frequently used in *Genere Diatonico* [diatonic modes],[79] not one out of a hundred simple organists will have an idea how to transpose each mode to C sharp, F sharp, G sharp, etc. Therefore, it is better to reserve the best temperament for the most used thirds.

What Boethius and other experienced ancient musicians have said will, most likely, continue to hold true, namely that musical harmony really is *Discors concordia* [conflicting concord]. Thus, this temperament must also incorporate variance, consistent with all of nature; one day is not quite so warm or cold as the next. In all, the aforementioned Zerlinius discusses specifically and separately three kinds of temperaments, first in *Institutionibus*, then in *Dialogis* and finally in *Suplementis* [sic].[80]

Someone might raise the point why, in my temperaments, I allow the false thirds, *e.g.* c sharp-f, F sharp-b flat, G sharp-c, to beat by nearly a comma, whereas Zarlinus has modified the scale by [tuning] the major thirds pure. To this I answer that in so doing Zarlinus did not [altogether] abandon *Scalam deatonam* [sic, the diatonic scale; *i.e.* the Pythagorean scale which employs pure fifths]. He merely wanted to demonstrate the possibility of casting major and minor thirds in certain harmonic ratios that might approach equal [temperament] more nearly than had previously been the case. Notwithstanding the greater deviation from equality [*i.e.* equal tempera-

---

[79]Here, presumably, transpositions of modes and keys to natural-key tonics.

[80]Werckmeister cites accurately enough Zarlino's *Le istitutioni harmoniche*, Venice, 1558, 1562, 1573; and *Sopplimenti musicali*, Venice, 1588. However, apparently once again relying on his memory, he commits the rather embarrassing error of ascribing to Zarlino the *Dialogo della musica antica et della moderna*, Florence, 1581, whose author and one time Zarlino pupil, Vincenzo Galilei (ca. 1520-91), differs considerably (and occasionally rather rudely) with his former teacher.

ment] in the ratios of thirds — major [thirds] having been larger by
one comma, minor [thirds] smaller by one comma — still, the ancients heard them not as dissonances but as consonances, as has been
confirmed by Faber Stapulensis, Glareanus and others.[81] *Videatur
Baryphonus Pleiade I, quaestione VI* [see also Chapter I, section
VI, of Baryphonus' *Pleiades*], where, once again, we can find [stated]
the reason why Barth. Ramus[82] and Zarlinus invented *Scalam Syn-
tonicam* [the syntonic scale]: certainly they did not envisage harmonic variability as the function of this scale, since the fifths d-a
would be one comma too small, and [the fourth] a-d one comma too
large, an intolerable [situation] for [purposes of] harmony. The
third f-a is also one comma too large, as was the case with the ancients, [and all] the other major thirds etc. [*i.e.* behave similarly].
Therefore, it is a poor expedient to reproach [me by arguing] that
Zarlinus modified the scale because its thirds had previously been
one [syntonic] comma, eighty-one eighteenths, too small or too large.
One may turn this matter inside out, there is no alternative, none
whatsoever, to [some kind of] temperament. Since, as has been asserted, the ancients' ears were perfectly happy with thirds all of which
were either too large or too small by one comma, one should really
be able to accept deviations one comma too large or too small, in
just a few rarely used thirds. And even if one wants to supply a keyboard with the conventional three or more *Subsemitonia* [double
keys], it still remains piecemeal patchwork which does not eliminate
the need for tempered tuning of the others [*i.e.* the remaining keys].
This seems to me like saying, Holy Scripture is imperfect unless

---

81 Jacobus Faber Stapulensis (ca. 1455-1537), influential French theologian, also humanistically interested in music. His *Elementa musicalia* is
based on and revises the theories of Boethius. — Heinrich Glareanus (1488-
1563), Swiss-German humanist and music theorist, who during his stay in
Paris (1517-22) was in close contact with Faber, is the author of the treatise
Dodekachordon.

82 According to Johann Gottfried Walther, *op. cit.*, Bartholomaeus Ramus,
a native Spaniard, taught in Bologna as "Professor Publicus in the *early
seventeenth* [my emphasis] century." Since Walther, somewhat skeptically,
reports Baryphonus' and Gafurius' (Franchinus Gaffurius, 1451-1522) credit-
ing Ramus with the "invention of the Scalae syotonae" (*sic*, syntonic scales)
one might have to read "early sixteenth" rather than seventeenth century.

supplied with marginal commentary; *sed Glossa speciosa fefellit* [but a slick phrase is always deceptive]. The *Subsemitonia* [double keys] have confused many a person. Yet, they will never be sufficient, even if one were to place one hundred of them into one single octave; *Natura ab infinitis abhorret* [A natural constitution shrinks away from the unlimited]. Even less [effectiveness can be expected] when there are only three [double keys] in an octave.

But should a person apply as much [temperament] as I have done — I wish to say this without claiming special merit — he will find out for himself what can be done [with it]. Some people argue that it is not customary to compose and arrange in all keys, *e.g.* c sharp, f sharp, g sharp. But I say, some people may not, but others may. Furthermore, even if one does not write in these keys *pare* [by denomination, *i.e.* using them as tonic], the progressions nevertheless may move onward [*i.e.* one may have to modulate] to such an extent as to render the *Subsemitonia* [double keys] insufficient. But how could I arrogate the right to set limits for one or the other [musicians] by forbidding him to write in a given key because the *Subsemitonia* [double keys] are not sufficiently effective!

The liberal arts want liberal minds. One cannot shackle or delimit them. For each has the liberty to act or not to act in accordance with the laws of nature and reason.

By way of conclusion, may God grant that all our work advance God's honor alone, and serve our neighbors' benefit that we may keep a pure and clean heart before God and our fellow man unto our

END.